CP 12⁵ᵗ

MAGNUS ON THE MOVE

"In the beginning . . ."

Magnus Magnusson on location at Uruk (Biblical Erech) in the ancient
land of Sumer. This was the cradle of civilisation as we know it.

MAGNUS
ON THE MOVE

MAGNUS MAGNUSSON

MACDONALD PUBLISHERS
EDINBURGH

© Magnus Magnusson 1980

ISBN 0 904265 40 4

Published by
Macdonald Publishers
Loanhead, Midlothian EH20 9SY

Printed in Scotland by
Macdonald Printers (Edinburgh) Limited
Edgefield Road, Loanhead, Midlothian EH20 9SY

CONTENTS

Acknowledgments

The Publishers would like to thank the following for supplying illustrations for *Magnus on the Move:*

David Collison, Producer, BBC London, for his own photographs on pages 56, 103, and for his help in locating many others.

The Daily Record, Glasgow, for the photographs on pages 22,40,86,125,133; Bord Fáilte, Dublin, page 154; James McBain of McBain, Tucson, page 68; Morgunbladid, Reykjavik and Òlafur K. Magnùsson, pages 74,78,79; Mexican National Tourism Office and A. G. Formenti, pages 28,31; National Tourist Organisation of Greece, pages 100,106; Egyptian Ministry of Tourism, pages 14,17; Italian State Tourist Office, London, pages 142,145; BBC London, *Frontispiece* and pages 50,54,104; Unilever Limited, pages 88-89.

Ray Henman, pages 61,119; John Tellick, page 116; Professor Thom, page 62.

J. Allan Cash Ltd, pages 19,34,37,128,136,137,148; Joya Hairs, Guatemala, pages 108,111,112; Robert Harding, London, pages 82,122; Mats Wibe Lund, Jr, Reykjavik, pages 151,152; National Museum, Dublin, pages 158,159.

INTRODUCTION

TRADITIONALLY, there are three Estates of the Realm: the Lords Spiritual, the Lords Temporal, and the Commons. To these have been added a Fourth Estate, and even a Fifth. I am a member of the last two.

It is said that the great parliamentarian Edmund Burke once pointed to the Press Gallery in the House of Commons and opined, "Yonder sits the Fourth Estate." To be sure, Brewer's *Dictionary of Phrase and Fable* primly points out that there is no written record that Burke ever said this. But the phrase, like all good phrases, stuck; and all journalists have ever since revelled in the illusion that they *are* the Fourth Estate. Brewer also adds that the BBC is sometimes known (jocularly) as the Fifth Estate.

So between them, the Fourth and Fifth Estates make up The Media.

But before those of us in The Media let it go to our heads, let us consider how Burke might have developed his theme—if he ever stated it. Surely he would have said that compared with the Lords Spiritual and the Lords Temporal, the Fourth Estate should be known as the "Lords Ephemeral"—and not Commons, but merely common. For what we deal with in what one journalist has splendidly called our "marvellously ignoble calling" is, quite simply, ephemera.

This little book is a collection of such ephemera.

The word "ephemeral," meaning "living for a day or only a few days," is derived from an order of exceptionally short-lived insects called Ephemeroptera. The usual example given in dictionaries is the mayfly, although a closer analogy in this particular context might be the gadfly ("an irritating or harassing insect or person").

Nor can it be a coincidence that the very word "journalist" echoes this concept of ephemerality, deriving as it does from the Latin *diurnalis*, meaning "of the day." It is the essence of journalism that it *should* be ephemeral.

This ephemerality is both a boon and a bane to journalists. Like gadflies, we are parasites—parasites of conflict: people who live off bad news and abhor the vacuum created by the opposite ("No news is good news"). As soon as the conflict is over, our part in reporting it, or helping to create it, is just as quickly forgotten, if not always forgiven.

We are gossips. And like all good gossips we have sharp eyes and sharp ears. We love a good story, and cannot wait to pass it on the moment we have heard it. "Gossip" is now a pejorative term; but I console myself by recalling that it derives from the Old English word *godsibb*, "godparent," or "a person related to one in God." When the word was first coined it implied a recognition of "gossip" as an essential ingredient of society, a kind of social cement.

But ephemerality is also a bane to journalists because in their overweening conceit they long for their work to endure. There is nothing sadder than a file of clippings of yellowing newsprint: yesterday's stories. And secretly in our hearts we would love our mortal words to be given the immortality of publication in a book.

A book such as this.

This book was not my idea, I hasten to say. It was suggested by one of the editors for whom I worked as a regular columnist on the magazine *Business Scotland*, Alwyn James. He did me the compliment of suggesting that some of the pieces I wrote for the magazine under his aegis were worth re-reading. Needless to say, I agreed with alacrity. Such is the vanity of journalists.

*   *   *

I have always considered myself a man of exceptional good luck, as they say in my beloved Icelandic Sagas. I am not particularly superstitious, but I have always been impressed by the certainty with which the Saga-writers of Iceland knew whether someone was "ill-starred" or "lucky." For them, "luck" was an essential element of destiny itself, something you were either born with, or not.

As an Icelander by birth (I was born in Reykjavik, of Icelandic parents, and migrated to Edinburgh at the age of nine months when my father was appointed European Manager of the Icelandic Co-op), I was nurtured on the Icelandic Sagas at my mother's knee. Night after night, she would tell me the stories enshrined in the great prose Sagas of the north, the story of Njal of Bergthorsknoll and the terrible burning in which he and his family died, the story of Gudrun in Laxdaela Saga and her agonized love-life, the story of Gunnlaug

Serpent-Tongue, the young Icelandic poet who told a king of Norway that "Men do not limp while their legs are the same length" (what a marvellous slogan with which to go through life!).

She also told me the story of how the name "Magnus" arose. It's buried in the depths of the *Saga of Saint Olaf*, one of the Sagas in the monumental *Heimskringla* (History of the Kings of Norway) written by the Icelandic historian Snorri Sturluson in the first half of the 13th century. The year was 1024. And King Olaf Haraldsson of Norway, later to be canonised as St Olaf of Norway, had clearly been doing a little sinning on the side, despite his posthumous sanctity. This is how Snorri Sturluson tells the story of how the Magnus name came about:

There was a woman called Alfhild, who was called the king's concubine; but she was of good birth, and very beautiful, and she was at King Olaf's court. That spring it became apparent that Alfhild was with child, and the king's confidants knew that he was the father. One night, Alfhild became ill and went into labour. There were few people at hand, just some women and a priest and an Icelander called Sighvat the Poet, and a few others. It was a very difficult birth, and Alfhild very nearly died. Eventually she gave birth to a boy-child, and for a while no one knew whether there was any life in the infant. But then at last the child started breathing, very weakly; and the priest asked Sighvat the Poet to go and tell the king.

Sighvat replied, "I don't dare to wake the king on any account, for he has forbidden anyone to disturb his sleep until he wakes up of his own accord."

The priest said, "But it is essential that the child should be baptised at once! I don't think it has any chance of surviving."

Sighvat replied, "Rather than wake the king, I would prefer to take the risk of baptising the child without his knowledge. I shall take the responsibility for giving him a name."

So the child was baptised, and christened—Magnus.

Next morning, when the king got up, he was told what had happened during the night, and thereupon had Sighvat the Poet summoned to his presence.

"How dare you," he said, "have my child baptised without my knowledge?"

"Because," replied Sighvat, "I preferred to give two souls to God, than one to the devil."

"What do you mean?" said the king, suspiciously.

Sighvat replied: "The child was at death's door, and would have belonged to the Devil if it had died unbaptised; but now it belongs to God. And secondly, I knew that if you were so angry with me for what I had done that my own life was at stake, I reckoned that if I lost my life on this account, I would belong to God also."

The king said, "But why did you name the boy *Magnus*? It is not a family name."

Sighvat replied, "I named him after the emperor Charlemagne, Charles Magnus, Charles the Great, for to my mind he is the greatest man the world has ever seen."

Whereupon the king said, "You are a man of great good luck, Sighvat. It's not surprising that good luck should accompany good brains; but it's strange that it should sometimes happen that good luck attends men without brains, to such an extent that witless schemes can turn out well!"

And with that, the king was now well pleased.

I'm glad to report that the boy did very well, despite his fraught beginnings, and eventually added lustre to the royal history of Norway as King Magnus the Good (1035-47). And with that, "Magnus" became a common and lucky name throughout the northlands, culminating in that Saint Magnus whose 12th century cathedral superintends the town of Kirkwall in the Orkneys.

The good luck of the Magnus name has attended me and my own "witless schemes" as well, throughout my career as a journalist and broadcaster. I have been enabled, by both the Fourth and Fifth Estates, to pursue my personal interest and passions and turn them into a profession, or at least a trade. They made me, in the very real sense of the term, a journeyman journalist. My insatiable thirst for gossip was given free play on the *Scottish Daily Express* and, later, *The Scotsman*. My curiosity about the gossip of the past as well as the present was given even more scope with the BBC—the Fifth Estate—and with the magazine *Scotland*, from which these ephemeral articles are culled.

I first started writing for *Business Scotland* (it was simply called

Scotland in those days) in 1964. That was the year that I first took up television seriously. I had done some documentaries and Arts programmes for BBC Scotland and a panel programme for STV called *Sense and Nonsense* as a sideline, but in 1964 I was invited to London to join Cliff Michelmore and the rest of the boys on the old *Tonight* programme of blessed memory.

At that time the editor of *Scotland* was a friend of mine, David Donald, who now runs his own PR consultancy business in Glasgow. We had got to know each other well when he had been Industrial Correspondent on *The Scotsman*, where I was then Chief Features Writer. *Scotland* was then the official publication of the Scottish Council (Development and Industry), serving the business community of Scotland. When David Donald heard that I was going to London, he asked me to contribute a monthly column about the people and places that I would be experiencing in the "big-time."

After the demise of *Tonight* in 1965, I returned to Scotland (I had been on a year's leave from *The Scotsman*), and continued to scratch out my monthly column. And then, in 1966, came what I will always look upon as the luckiest break in my lucky career: I was asked by the late Paul Johnstone to help him develop and present a monthly TV programme on history and archaeology to be called *Chronicle*. Paul Johnstone had already made television history as the inventor and producer of the immensely successful archaeological quiz game called *Animal, Vegetable, Mineral?* back in the 1950s, starring Professor Glyn Daniel and Sir Mortimer Wheeler. Now, as head of a new Archaeological and Historical Unit, he was looking for someone with experience in current affairs to front the programmes that he hoped would make the "dead" world of the past topical.

For the next ten years I quartered the world for *Chronicle* as a free-lance presenter. I am neither an archaeologist nor a historian by training, but I found myself developing an overwhelming interest in the subject—an interest that eventually expressed itself in even more ambitious projects like *BC: The Archaeology of the Bible Lands* and, more recently, *Vikings!*

These travels for *Chronicle* (and other occasional programmes) took me all over the archaeological world as we perceived it then. They took me to Egypt, the Land of the Pharoahs, a land for which I formed a deep and exasperated affection; to Easter Island with its mysterious statues; to Tonga and the South Sea islands in search of a living model for our own past; to Iceland, of course, which still and always tugs at my heart (my wife says that I am an Icelander by birth but Scotch by absorption!); to China, just when it was opening itself again to the West after the trauma of the Cultural Revolution of 1966 (I was one of the first Western journalists to be allowed into the country in 1973); to Central America, in search of the marvellous lost civilisation of the Maya; to the Mediterranean, looking for lost Atlantis on the volcanic island of Santorini, north of Crete; to Ireland, to Greenland, to the Hebrides, to Paradise itself in the Persian Gulf ("Sandalwood for my beard").

Throughout those globe-trotting years I would send my monthly column from every corner of the world (I think I only missed my deadline once, although I stand to be corrected by Alwyn James). They would be scribbled on aeroplanes, typed in trains, scrawled in notebooks in between bouts of filming. They weren't intended to be a summary of whatever script I was working on for the BBC at the time; rather, they were impressions of the places I was fortunate enough to visit by courtesy of the BBC, impressions now imprisoned in the amber of memory.

* * *

Whenever a writer commits words to paper, he instantly regrets them. When he sees them in print, he instantly realises how he could have written them better. He wants to start re-writing, re-arranging, re-structuring, trying to improve, to polish, to embellish. This is an especial temptation when the prospect looms of the ephemeral being granted a new lease of life.

Should I "up-date" the articles? Should I change the tenses to make them sound as if they were being written now and not a few years ago? And would that not give me a chance of sneaking in a few "improvements," like parliamentarians who are allowed to polish the form of what they said, in *Hansard*? The temptation was particularly powerful because of my love for words themselves. I think I have always had a love-affair with dictionaries, with bluff words and brazen words, glutton words and starveling words, gruff words and tender words. There is nothing I like better than a Chambers under my bed. And so I feel an acute sense of responsibility towards words. If I have misused them, I regret it; if I have abused them, I mourn it. A sense of inadequacy, even of shame, impels me to try to do penance for sinning against syntax. The opportunity to reprint can also offer a heaven-sent opportunity to re-write.

After considerable discussion it was decided that these *obiter dicta*, these "sayings by the way," should go in unchanged. Where I thought the reader should know of some significant development, like the death of the subject of an article, I have added a footnote. But nothing else. However, my editor, Alwyn James, has taken it upon himself to remove one or two "insider" references, like the obsession I had with trying to get the world to give up smoking with me.

So here they stand, plain and unadorned: a fleeting record of three golden years at the start of the 1970s when the whole world was my oyster—and my hunger for oysters knew no bounds. They were marvellous years, when the horizons of my mind were stretched with every new journey. And it was good to have an editor like Alwyn James, long-suffering and resigned, who allowed me to write on any subject that interested *me*—with the proviso that I would hear soon enough if it ceased to interest *him*. I owe a great debt of gratitude to him, and to the other editors for whom I wrote in *Scotland/Business Scotland*.

I would dearly like to think that the articles I wrote then in the flush and fury of the moment still retain a certain validity, and still express a certain truth, despite their ephemerality.

1

Relaxing in the Valley of Kings

I SAT THERE, just watching. Watching and brooding. The sun was hot on my back, on the nape of my neck. January sun. Great, just great. And I was watching this ant.

Some way behind my chair he had found a large lump of dry dung; and he was now in the process of lugging it home. Lugging it, did I say? Sometimes I got the impression that it was lugging him. He hauled, heaved, shoved, bounced, rolled, slid, tugged; sometimes cartwheeling it, dragging it into the deep gullies of footprints in the dust, sometimes panting with it up the steep slope of a wheel-mark. But never giving up. Never slowing down. Intent, totally intent, on getting the thing home. Oblivious to everyone and everything else. . . .

Oblivious, for instance, to the fact that there was a pied wagtail, just like the kind we get here in Britain—a pied wagtail foraging for its breakfast 15 or 20 feet ahead. For my part there was no conscious moment of realisation; no moment when I said to myself, "Hey, that little ant's for the chop!" There was just this physical awareness that the ant and the wagtail were going to meet, and then. . . .

And then. A couple of leisurely strides or hops. A quick dart of movement. The ant no more. I went across to the spot. I could make out in the dust the little forked prints of the wagtail. But I couldn't find the piece of dung. Had the bird eaten that, too? I hoped not. I hoped it had been left somewhere for the next ant to pick up the torch. . . .

It had a curiously profound effect on me, that little scene. There was I, sitting at my ease in Egypt in between bouts of filming at Luxor, in the Valley of the Kings; and suddenly seeing a whole parable of Egypt, of the Middle East, in a momentary encounter between an ant and a wagtail. I began to see how easy it is to develop a fatalistic, even mechanistic, view of life here under the Egyptian sun. It teaches you philosophy. After all that heroic endeavour, the ant was snuffed out, and no one cared. I thought of these generations of Egyptian labourers who had toiled to produce these monstrous tombs of the mighty. I thought of the teeming millions of Cairo, little boys clinging perilously on the back of trams amidst some of the most frenetic traffic I've ever seen in my life. Human life . . . ants . . . sun . . . indolence . . . yes, why not?

It's such a deplorable, likeable, infuriating, fascinating country, Egypt. It's so goddam inefficient, in the first place. The street-lights of Cairo are dim, dim (except for the mosque where Nasser lies buried). So why not light the place properly with all that new power from the Aswan dam, you fulminate, feeling your way along the dingy streets?

The trains don't work, in a diabolically subtle way. You see, the British laid the line up the Nile; but the rolling-stock on it comes from the Hungarian Railway Carriage & Machine Works, Györ—and its gauge is a quarter of an inch narrower. So all the way, on the endless overnight journey from Cairo to Luxor, the carriage-wheels were hunting the gauge, side to side, interminably, until you felt sure the wheels were square.

Oh, yes, and I caught a flea. Or at least, a flea caught me.

High in the blue sky, a pair of kites plane in endless circles, drifting on a midday thermal. Doves with white-barred tails court their girls with aggressive hunched shoulders along the avenue of sphinxes. This eternally deplorable place, that squandered so much of its wealth and potential on these great empty monuments to a ruler's megalomania!

And has it changed? All these tanks we saw? All the armaments? It all seems so unreal, compared with Egypt itself.

The dust. All that dust. Strange to think that it started off as being mountain in Ethiopia; before the scouring Nile took it and floated it down the stream, and spread it lovingly as life-giving silt in Upper Egypt; and the winds dry it, and blow it, and waste it.

And what will happen now that the Aswan Dam has been built? Will the life-giving silt get past, the silt that nourishes that barren land and keeps the millions fed? And if it can't get past, will all the new-won electricity have to go on manufacturing fertiliser to replace the silt that the dam is blocking? It would not surprise me. It's a contrary place, Egypt.

Visitors at the entrance to the Temple of Luxor

And soon, so very soon, you find yourself getting less and less exasperated. So something doesn't work? So what? Does it really matter all that much? Will it make all that difference tomorrow, or the next day, or the next? And they grin at you, these fine happy open dishonest faces, and your exasperation melts.

One thing at least you feel right from the start; and that is the sensation of travelling. Air travel has spoilt travelling, for the most part. It isn't travelling when you stroll on at one end of the tube and get squeezed out the other, hours later, in a different world. But in Egypt, you can still recapture the heady delights of real Victorian travel.

You've got to have Cook's, of course. And preferably a lot of luggage, like a film unit with full gear (43 pieces). The Cook's men take over. What a Babel! Porters are boldly tongue-lashed, bystanders are driven from the path, officials are squared and soothed, there is a yelling and a shouting, a sprightly caravan of dark-skinned men in night-shirts and vast bedcaps humping luggage, cleaving a way along crowded platforms, forming up to take undisputed possession of the best sleeping berths: Cook's have booked it. And you distribute largesse or bakshish with a lordly hand, and feel, for once, privileged and unguilty.

For tipping, which I loathe, suddenly begins to make sense in Egypt. It's pointless to make a song and dance about servility and humiliation and indignity; these concepts simply don't enter into it. There is no social welfare in Egypt; it is the function of the well-to-do to distribute social benefits amongst the less well-to-do, in the form of endless tips. For a small child to come and pester you for money is as natural as for a woman in Britain to go into a Post Office to draw her Children's Allowance.

Nor should one get upset about the apparent altercations that go on all the time. Organisation, in Egypt, is carried out at the top of one's voice, rather crossly, but without ill humour. It's just a way of speaking. It has no more malice in it than the automatic beating that everyone deals out to the wretched donkeys. Thwack, thwack, shout, shout: punctuation marks, that is all.

And the sun goes down in a thunderously flaming red—very quickly, much more abruptly than at home, one feels; and the sunset has hardly time to fade before the rush-hour traffic has got its headlights on, all jostling and hustling and endlessly sounding their horns; but not in anger. Just to express themselves, console themselves maybe; prove that they exist. Aural worry-beads.

For I think *that,* probably, is one of the main problems in Egypt—proving that you exist as a person, not just an ant. You look at some of the young men: superbly handsome faces, masculine faces, full of a brooding, scowling power or the sunshine of laughter. And you think to yourself, what has a young man like that got to look forward to? How is he going to express his manhood? In a relentless attrition of nationality against Israel? How will he fulfil himself? On bakshish? Selling phoney antiques to tourists in the Ethiopian dust?

There was a pair of railway-bogey wheels lying on the ground where we were filming. It looked heavy as lead. The young men, these bright-faced sometimes scowling young men, amused themselves by picking it up with one hand, hoist, straight up. And laughed with delight at our admiration.

Herding goats in the Valley of Kings

And somehow in the dust, tended by squads of able-bodied young men, the well-watered Red Canna Lilies flaunt their heads. Pink oleanders, scarlet poinsettias, bougainvillea everywhere, hibiscus glowing velvet in the shade. So welcome to the winter-jaundiced eye. And soon you even stopped worrying about that, too. And about the ancient tombs. For there was nothing morbid about them. Down the long galleries of the tomb of Rameses II, the decorative carvings blaze with colour and life, yes—life. And the ruins, these extravagant wasteful ruins seem to come to life, too. More so than the ruins of classical Greece—don't ask me why, I cannot explain it. And you realise that this deplorable country is beginning to take hold of you, hypnotise you; and you start to understand why so many archaeologists have fallen under its spell and devoted their lives to Egyptology under the burning sun.

The incongruities remain: the bubbling cheer and the sense of fatalism; the merry optimism and the knowledge of defeat; the shrewd intelligence and the wilful ignorance; the kindness and the gross incompetence.

And you sigh, and shrug, and turn another side to the sun. And reflect that there can be few nicer places in the world in January than Luxor by the Nile. Tea on the terrace while the sun goes down in thunder and the horse-drawn carriages patter by, and the currency-racket boys haunt the street outside like kites planing in the midday thermals. . . .

Funny place, Egypt. It gets you, somehow.

March, 1971

2

The Day I Met Two Mermaids

THE ISLAND OF Raasay, Skye's own little offshore island, has been hitting the headlines with a general stushie of threats and accusations flying around concerning the activity (or inactivity) of the island's owner, one Dr Green: "Dr No," as the media have dubbed him.

No matter how excited most of the island's inhabitants become, two large, fat, female residents had seen it all before. There must have been an air of "Oh, no—not again!" in the set of their massive heads—that is if they still have their heads intact after all these years. The last I heard of them they were looking decidedly the worse of wear. And that must have been twenty years earlier, long before all this talk of absentee landlords, and schemes to build a ferry, and trouble over salmon fishing rights. Raasay House was a hotel and nobody had heard of Dr Green, the English doctor who now owns the house and most of the island but never lives there.

It was a great day for Raasay, that warm summer afternoon in 1951 when the two large maidens gazed stonily out to sea and saw a motor boat approaching from the neighbouring island of Skye. It was packed to the gunwales with folk in kilts and tartan and summer frocks and a piper played them across the water. Raasay had never had so many visitors in its life—if you discount the hordes of red-jackets who came over with Cumberland to plunder the wee island after the '45.

Ah but this was different. This was the fleshpots for Raasay. Up till then Big Sister Skye had had all the fun and excitement.

The young folk of Raasay had to cross to Skye for a late-night dance, or a concert or a film show. And all the rich tourists went to Skye, which was even then in the middle of one of its annual Skye Weeks, with streams of exiled Scots coming from all over the world to visit the land of their forefathers and have tea with Dame Flora Macleod of Macleod at Dunvegan Castle.

But in a fit of magnanimity in Festival of Britain Year, 1951, Skye decided to give a day of glory to Raasay, and creamed off a boatload of her own tourists to visit the small island. The guest of honour was a Raasay descendant from Australia, called Dr Macleod, and the Press went along to record the occasion.

Tea was set out in the garden of Raasay House Hotel, and the highlight was to be a display of country dancing by a team of young folk who had been training hard all winter under the guidance of the Further Education officer and the more than slightly disapproving eye of their elders who thought all this exhibitionism was a wee thing sinful.

But as it happened it wasn't the dancers or the return of the exile that stole the day. It was the two large maidens. They were the first sight to meet the eyes as the boat came into the landing on the shore beneath Raasay House.

And what a sight—two large, no not large, gargantuan stone mermaids, just sitting there, alone on the beach, noses chipped, ears missing, bosoms broken, faces pitted and scarred by the lashing seas.

What on earth were they? The reporters couldn't wait to get

Raasay House in some disarray

ashore and find out. Never mind the dancers. The tea could wait. Who could tell them about the mermaids?

They were directed to the house of John Macleod and when they met John Macleod and heard his story they began to take a new interest in Raasay, to realise it was something more than just an off-beat place to patronise for an afternoon and write a few funny paragraphs about for the diary column.

Raasay was history, and real people—people like John Macleod who was a kind of uncrowned king of Raasay. He was just a crofter. But his little house was crammed to the ceiling with books in many languages. He was a scholar in English as well as his native Gaelic. He was steeped in philosophy, and over-flowing with history and skilled at law. When crofters on a neighbouring island had been arrested for staking land claims in 1920 he had fought their case in court and won on a point of law.

He was the local cobbler, registrar, district clerk, land officer, special constable, librarian, councillor, and I can't remember how many other things. He had umpteen strapping sons and daughters in high positions—police chiefs, hospital matrons and suchlike—all over Britain. The blond kilted giant who had tied the visitors' boat up at the jetty was John's youngest son, on holiday from some university or other.

So when John Macleod told the story of the Raasay mermaids none of those hard-necked reporters doubted one word of it.

It all went back, John said, to the '45 rebellion, in which the Macleods of Raasay were on the side of the Young Pretender.

And here John interrupted his flow to make sure that nobody was labouring under any mistaken notion that the Raasay Macleods had anything to do with the Skye Macleods.

"We are an entirely separate clan from that of Dame Flora of Dunvegan. We have our own tartan—the black and yellow Macleod, sometimes known as the Dress Macleod."

Yes, he was aware that Dame Flora sometimes wore the Dress Macleod tartan, as well as the Macleod of Lewis and the Ancient tartan. Sometimes—and he gave a kind of shiver of horror—she even wore all three *AT ONCE!*

"She's a very nice lady," he said. "But she has really no right to wear the Raasay tartan."

Anyway, the point was that whereas the Dunvegan Macleods had sided with the Government in the '45, little Raasay had fought for Prince Charlie, and when it was all over the Duke of Cumberland had taken his vengeance and burned the Raasay chief's house to the ground.

The Macleod had to build a new Raasay House and he decided that he would like two stone mermaids, one on either side of the front door. He commissioned an architect to see to the details but specified that he would like the mermaids to be the size of large dogs.

The house was finished and one day a boat came staggering across the water and dumped two stone mermaids on the beach.

Poor Macleod was flabbergasted when he saw the monstrous maids. Apart from the problem of getting them up the steep rocky road to the house, there was the distinct possibility that once these large lassies were in position nobody would be able to see the house.

He told the architect to take them away and bring a smaller pair. The architect, thanking his lucky stars the boat hadn't sunk on the way over, had no intention of risking a return voyage in the same company.

"You ordered them, you've got 'em," he said. "They stay here."

"Right," said Macleod, who hadn't defied the Bloody Butcher Cumberland to be frightened by some twopence-ha'penny architect, "I refuse to pay for them."

"Right," said the architect, "I'll take you to court."

And he did. Macleod fought the case, maintaining that he had ordered mermaids as big as dogs, and until someone could produce a dog as big as the monstrosities on his beach, he was within his rights in witholding payment.

Well, they found such a dog. Witnesses swore to the existence of an Italian mountain dog as big as the Raasay mermaids. Macleod had to pay damages as well as all the costs of the case (including, I suppose, the dog-hunting safari in the Alps).

He was ruined, had to sell his new house, and emigrate to Australia. The Dr Macleod visiting Raasay that day in 1951 was the first descendant of the ruined chief to return to the island.

He seemed to find the vast mermaids very funny and didn't bear them any grudge for sending his family to the Antipodes.

Whether he was better off out there than John Macleod, another descendant, crofter, librarian, scholar, philosopher on a tiny island, is another matter.

But if those mermaids are still on Raasay—and I can't imagine what could ever remove them, apart from an atom bomb—then I'm sure they have a long-suffering look on their battered faces.

In matters of litigation, foreign invasion, visiting doctors, stubborn property owners and storms blowing round Raasay House—they have seen it all before. . . .

Having said all that, I must admit I couldn't resist trying to find out if those mermaids really are still on Raasay. So I contacted the island post office and a cheery voice assured me that the two old girls are still large as life on their island fastness.

What's more, so is John Macleod, hale and hearty and 89 years old. He wasn't exactly on Raasay when I phoned. He had nipped across to Inverness for a holiday with one of his married daughters, and by the time I contacted her, he had left for Bridge of Allan to stay with his son Norman, who is Chief Superintendent of police in Stirling.

Two other sons live on Raasay—John, a retired head forester, and Murdo, a retired police inspector. There's a married daughter on Raasay, and two in Inverness. Scotty, the fair-haired giant who charmed the visitors in 1951, is a veterinary surgeon in Australia, and another son is a doctor.

John confirmed that the mermaids are still intact, but he was sorry to say the cannon had been removed. I had forgotten about them. Apparently the Raasay folk set a couple of cannon up on the beach during the Napoleonic Wars in case the Frenchies tried on any of Cumberland's capers.

Whether it was the mermaids who scared them off I don't know, but the invasion never came and Raasay was left with another couple of white elephants.

But it just goes to show that when Raasay folk decide to take action they are a force to be reckoned with.

"We're slow to rouse," said Mrs Macdonald, one of the Inverness daughters. "There's a lot of murmuring for a long time, but when Raasay folk finally make themselves heard they really mean business.

"My father no longer serves on committees, but his mind is still very active and people respect his opinion. No doubt he'll get caught up in all the goings-on in Raasay when he gets back."

And when will that be?

"When he hears the first cuckoo he'll be off to Raasay," said his daughter-in-law.

Yes, landlords may come and go, but John Macleod always comes back to Raasay. A Macleod of Macleod if ever there was one, king of his island, custodian of its history, as immovable as the stone maidens who welcome him home.

April, 1972

John Macleod came back to Raasay for the last time in March, 1975. He died in Portree Hospital in Skye, and now lies buried in his beloved Raasay. His mantle has been taken over by his son Murdo, the retired police inspector, who is now chairman of Raasay Community Council. The land owned by Dr Green, including Raasay House, has now been bought by the Highlands and Islands Development Board; the main house is to be turned into an Adventure School, the Annexe (Borrodale House) into a 15-bedroomed hotel.

And the mermaids are still there, bless them.

3

To the Halls of Moctezuma

MEXICO CITY is a truly astounding place. Booming? That's simply inadequate to describe the bustling explosion of teeming urban life that goes on here. Mexico City is now the sixth largest city in the world, and growing . . . and growing. Its population has increased by 35 per cent in the past ten years. It has now topped the 8 million mark. The population of the country as a whole, now 50 million, will be over 70 million by the end of the 'seventies, and will burst the 100 million barrier by the end of the century.

Mexico is rich, although most of the peasants are still poor. Mexico City is rich: at least, a lot of Mexico Citizens are rich, many of them very rich indeed. I dined once in one of those palatial suburban haciendas: servants galore, gardeners galore, it was like being right back in the Edwardian age. The money comes from steel, from oil, from cars. Every year, production records are smashed. Every year, thousands of Mexicans are surf-riding into the nouveau-riche middle-class on the crest of a roaring consumer bonanza.

Which came as a faint surprise, I must admit. I had had a hazy idea that the Spanish Conquistadores had cleaned the place out of all its gold and silver and jade when they over-threw the great, glittering civilisation of the Aztec and the Maya, and left the country oppressed and backward and poverty-stricken (which they did up to a point—I just hadn't bargained for what Mexico has done for itself since the Revolution of 1910). And I also had the vague notion that Mexico City had been practically custom-built to house the '68 Olympics and the '70 World Cup.

I think it was the celebrated new subway system that gave that

The Classic Period of the Maya in Mexico: the Temple of the Warriors at Chichen Itza in the Yucatan Peninsula

impression. It was inaugurated just before the Olympic Games, at such a mind-boggling number of millions of pesos that the French contractors are still waiting for many of the bills to be paid.

But what a thing of joy and beauty it is: elegant marble stations still spotlessly clean (even the Mexicans, that great race of champion spitters, have learned to refrain from spitting in their beloved Metro), decorated with lavish carvings in high relief. They are already building extension lines, which doesn't surprise me; there seems to be hardly any public transport above ground at all, apart from an enchanting system of taxis called "peseros" which ply up and down the main thoroughfares and on which you can ride as far as you like for one peso (about three new pence).

Down in the subway, you really are down amongst the roots of Mexico's long and exotic history. When they were excavating for one of the stations, Pino Suarez, they came across a buried Aztec temple on its pyramid. It's a small one, but is now enshrined as the centrepiece of the concourse. For Mexico City was built slap on top of the old Aztec capital of Tenochtitlan, which Hernando Cortez and his handful of beardless youths and horses had captured by a typical Old World mixture of guile and daring and deceitfulness and violence.

He was divinely aided, was Cortez—but not by the True God his soldier-priests had come to proclaim. It was the Aztec gods themselves who helped him. For the Aztec ruler, Moctezuma II, had been persuaded by the cruel oracles of his time that gods would arrive from the east in the guise of strange white mortals—and so he naïvely welcomed the Spaniards to his capital. It wasn't quite as easy as all that for Cortez, of course. Although Moctezuma was a fatalist, his people weren't, and in the end the Spaniards had to fight for their lives for two years before Tenochtitlan was taken. To the Aztec, these strange men discharging firearms from horses (which they had never seen) seemed like death-dealing Centaurs. Their arrows bounced harmlessly off metal breast-plates, spears and axes of obsidian shattered on swords of steel. The temples were overthrown, the gods of the air and the land, the plumed serpent, the eagle and the jaguar—all were trampled under these terrifying hooves into the dust of history.

(But Moctezuma, you might say, is getting his own back. They call it "Moctezuma's Revenge," the "Tenochtitlan Two-Step," or "turista," a sharp affliction of the guts caused by the indiscreet drinking of unpurified water).

The Conquest of Mexico, the rape of the New World by the Old, has always seemed to me to be one of the most poignant moments in history. And one which it is difficult to feel neutral about. "New World" was as much a misnomer as Columbus's ludicrous name of "Indians" for the natives he encountered, due to the geographical mirage he believed he had found—the West Indies. There had been people living in Mexico for 20,000 years before the Spaniards arrived. When the cavemen of Europe were painting their images on the Lascaux caves, Middle America was being populated. Long before the Indians of the East had transmitted the concept of a mathematical zero through the Arabs to European scholars, the Maya had worked it out for themselves. The Maya had also established a solar calendar of 365 days and a fraction, which was much more precise than the Gregorian calendar of 1582. Long before Archbishop Ussher was pontificating that the world had been created in the year 4,004 BC, the Maya knew that it was at least 125 million years old.

Even the Maya, whose great classical period was over by 1200 AD, were in decline before the Spaniards arrived. They had been superseded by the Toltec and the Aztec, a warrior race from the north, who introduced to the dreaming astronomer-priests of the Maya the savage barbarities of human sacrifice. Instead of time, the native Mexicans now worshipped blood and death in order to create life. Sacrificial victims had their hearts ripped from their bodies to give strength to the sun and to the plumed serpent.

Compared with the civilisation they overthrew, the Spanish civilisation was parvenu and backward, mercenary and unartistic. Its priests were appalled at the savage ceremonials to placate the gods—yet during the Inquisition they were to act with no less savagery and disregard of human life. In the name of progress and peace and profit (most especially profit), an alien race of adventurers came and battered this proud and ancient people not just into submission but into extinction. If the Aztec were the Romans of Middle America compared with the more graceful Greeks, the Maya, then the Spaniards were the Huns and the Visigoths tearing and looting and plundering for self-advancement.

There are some 11,000 listed archaeological sites in Mexico, and probably twice as many as that actually exist. It shows how remarkable was this civilisation that was destroyed. Many of the sites are engulfed in tropical jungle, trees growing from the roofs of mouldering temples, perhaps only a slab or two of incised stone or broken hieroglyphic to betray what was once a great ceremonial centre. And the wheel continues going round: for this great civilisation is once again being plundered, for greed and profit, by armed bands of smugglers who sell the carved stones to wealthy private collectors and dealers and museums at fantastic prices (a lump of carved stone can fetch up to $50,000).

But the tide has turned, I think. Cortez razed the city of Tenochtitlan and built upon the flattened rubble the embryonic Mexico City. Mexico became New Spain, and everywhere in Mexico City and the country itself you see traces of the Colonial style of architecture they imported. The huge city-centre Zocalo, the "Plaza de la Constitucion," is bounded by the massive baroque cathedral, the old Viceroy's palace—and the National Pawn Shop.

The Square of the Three Cultures, Mexico City

The colonial architecture is disappearing fast, and so too is the "Conquest mentality." For instance, although Mexico is still formally a Catholic country, the power of the church, a potent ally in the colonial days, has been severely trimmed and its wealth and lands taken from it. No Cabinet minister, however devout, may attend church during his term of office, for the church is disestablished. Up north in the Yucatan there are still a million Maya living in villages in the forests or cultivating maize in the burnt clearings, who still speak the old Maya language and still remember the old Maya gods: the Catholic church has never penetrated very deeply into their age-old native culture and ritual memories.

Today, modern Mexico is constantly renewing and rediscovering itself in terms of its past. The emphasis is all on its pre-Spanish origins, the mysterious, abstract world of the Maya with their labyrinthine symbolism and the martial world of the Aztec, the world of the eagle and the plumed serpent: this strange inheritance of opposites, of the grandiose and the delicate, the violent and the refined.

The Spanish period is tactfully or tacitly ignored. For instance, in Mexico City there is an equestrian statue of one of the Spanish emperors but now bearing the apologia that it has not been retained in a public place in order to honour the Spanish throne, but because of its artistic and aesthetic qualities. The vast frescoes that cover the soaring walls of the new University buildings are Indian in inspiration. So are the monumental sculptures, as primitive as Henry Moore's.

It is not that the Mexicans resent the Spanish occupation, for history is ineluctable—should one resent the Toltec and Aztec conquerors of the Maya? It is simply that the post-Conquest history of Mexico is an agonised struggle to find a true national identity. To be Mexican now is to be an extraordinary and fascinating blend of races and cultures which they rightly claim is unique and has a unique contribution to make to the world.

May, 1972

4

Sandalwood for my Beard and Rosewater for my Hands

I NEVER THOUGHT I would make it to the court of a real, live, absolute feudal monarch, as absolute and all-powerful as any Tudor on the throne of England. Nor did I think, despite the telly programmes on Henry VIII, that it would be paradise. But I did, and it was. In a manner of speaking, anyway.

It started with a kiss on the bridge of the nose. This, it seemed, was the appropriate if bizarrely intimate way to greet His Highness Shaikh Isa ben Sulman Al Khalifah, Ruler of Bahrein and its Dependencies, a pleasant, round, chubby little man of somewhat awesome power. I didn't go into just how much power, but I suspect it included detaching my head from my shoulders if the fancy took him.

We were ushered into the audience chamber just before 9 in the morning. There were half a hundred of us or more, and we weren't so much ushered in as pulled along in a slipstream. Shaikh Isa had arrived in a vast limousine that drew up outside his official residence. We were all waiting outside. A few favoured ones, who were relatives or close friends, were permitted a kiss on the imperial nose. Others, if sponsored by someone in authority, were granted a handshake. The rest just touched his clothes, feasted their eyes—and followed mutely when the shaikh moved across the court-yard into the long audience chamber.

There were seats right round the walls. The shaikh sat on a sofa in the middle of the far wall. Newcomers would sometimes be greeted formally with a wave of the hand, at which they withdrew to seats at the side, or else the shaikh would put out the cigarette he invariably

Wash-day on Bahrein

carries reeking in a holder and get to his feet. At which everyone had to get to their feet.

"It is good exercise for you," said His Highness Shaikh Isa ben Sulman Al Khalifah out of the corner of his mouth, and I warmed to him.

The formality was enchanting. Every five minutes or so, four attendants would sweep silently in with great copper kettles of tea or coffee, and bunches of cups. These they would hand out rapidly, pouring the sweetened tea in a deft and practised movement, while another waited to take your cup for use further down the line (only the shaikh's cup was not used again). The coffee that alternated was strongly flavoured with cardamom and saffron. It never occurs to you to refuse these relays of bracers.

The purpose of this morning audience is to give the shaikh's people access to the fount of decision. Any one of Bahrein's 200,000 inhabitants has the right to come to audience with a petition. He is waved forward by the Vizier (a man wearing the most formidable dagger I have ever seen), kneels before his shaikh (but not cravenly—more a matter of confidentiality, on one knee rather than both), whispers to him and leaves a letter. Sometimes the shaikh reads it and scribbles a comment there and then; or else lays it to one side.

Thus he operates as a kind of Ombudsman, for although there is naturally a government of ministers, Shaikh Isa's power is absolute. There is no income tax in Bahrein—the governmental income all comes from oil royalties and customs dues; and it is the Privy Purse alone which can dispense financial justice to the wronged or the unfortunate who present themselves at the morning Majlis, or audience.

To signify the end of the audience, the team of attendants come sweeping back, this time bearing pitchers of rosewater and braziers of burning sandalwood. The rosewater is for your hands; the burning sandalwood for your beard. At least you leave the Shaikh's presence smelling nice, your beard soft with the heady perfumed aroma of the smoke of sandalwood. It's a marvellous custom, and one that should be taken up for the slightest occasion.

The same thing happens at the end of the shaikh's private dinners (actually, they're rather public, but they're not, unlike his Majlis, open to all and sundry; at least not all the time). They are quite a test, these occasions—a test of sheer stamina and speed. The great tables are strewn with the carcasses of sheep and fowl, vast platters of vegetables and meats of every possible description. The idea is to eat as much as you can in as short a period as you can, for the shaikh doesn't loiter at table. An inveterate smoker (he is also on a diet) he gets bored with it all fairly quickly, and you are lucky if you reach the sweet by the time he's on his feet. And at that, of course, everyone has to be on his feet, and that's it. No sooner is the room cleared than the hangers-on—servants, drivers, and so on—are allowed in to clear the table (literally, like locusts). Some say darkly that amongst them are the chefs of the local hotels. Within ten minutes, there's not a scrap of food to be seen.

But why paradise? No paradise for ardent socialists, surely. But then, there don't seem to be many of them around; there hasn't been a revolution in years, and the last one was rather a quiet and bloodless affair which petered out after an attempt to blackmail the government by strikes. No, Bahrein, perhaps because it is an island in the Persian Gulf and not so accessible to Arab politics as other states, is stable and seems on the surface at least to be reasonably content. Its large oil income (large by the standards of any other community of its size, but relatively small compared with the income of some of the oil states) enables it to have fine roads, good buildings, and educational opportunity. There is the looming problem of confederation once the British "presence" is removed, and the ever-present danger of political infiltration, but apart from that Bahrein seems rather an idyllic sort of place; it has all the charm of Arab countries as well as the efficiency and living amenities inculcated by years of British and European affinity.

But that's not really what I meant by paradise. I meant it more literally than that. For the island of Bahrein seems to have been the model, or at least the prototype, of the Garden of Eden.

There have been many claimants to this exalted position. Favourite has always been the area of ancient Mesopotamia between the Tigris and Euphrates, the fertile crescent from which the Biblical tribes originally sprang. The Garden of Eden, in the old view, was a folk memory of those green places affectionately recalled in the burning heat of the desert wanderings.

But now an English archaeologist called Geoffrey Bibby has questioned this view and produced thought-provoking evidence to

Beached on Bahrein

suggest that Eden was part of a complex chain of myth and legend originating in the Persian Gulf itself, on Bahrein.

His work is all part of a large movement which is opening up the past to us at a remarkable rate, bringing to our knowledge civilisations that had been totally lost to us or survived only as obscure Biblical names.

One such civilisation was that of "Dilmun." For 2,500 years its very name was lost to history—yet once it had been a household name throughout the ancient Middle East, as a thriving and important trading centre and as a place of legend. The name only came to light again when archaeologists began to uncover the lost civilisations of Assyria and Babylonia—and even then it was simply a name. A reference to a place of trading.

But the most tantalising references were to Dilmun as the Garden of the Gods; a paradisal area where fresh water was everywhere to be found, where there was always peace and happiness and fertile growth. This was the place, for instance, to which the Sumerian equivalent of Noah was sent after the Flood as a reward—the only human being to have been endowed with immortality.

And it was in search of this immortality that Gilgamesh, hero of the Sumerian "Epic of Gilgamesh," comes to Dilmun to consult "Noah." And Noah tells him he must pluck the flower of immortality from the sea-bed by tying stones to his feet and sinking down through the sea. Gilgamesh does so, plucks the flower (a symbol for a pearl), and goes to his room; but while he sleeps, a snake comes in and swallows the pearl. Thus, it is the snake that learns the secret, not man, and simply sloughs off his old skin whenever he gets old.

Geoffrey Bibby discovered some fascinating parallels when he started uncovering the prehistoric remains beneath the sands of Bahrein. He quickly established that it had been an extremely large and important trading centre; he found the remains of a huge palace and city near the capital.

He also found, in the floor of the palace, a number of funerary urns. These all had the skeleton of a snake inside—and one pearl. So the memory, at least, of a snake/immortality cult associated with Dilmun flourished in Bahrein.

Then that little flower of immortality. Well, one of the geological features of the area is that the water-table of Arabia comes almost to the surface at and around Bahrein. It has copious fresh water—even on the sea-bed! Springs break through the sea-bed and you can dive down and fill a bag with fresh water in the middle of the sea. And the oyster beds are found near the springs. . . . What's more, the pearl fishermen of Bahrein to this very day tie stones to their feet to get down to the bottom.

Slowly, a pile of circumstantial evidence is beginning to accumulate (in Dilmun, for instance, one of the healing gods was called the Lord of the Rib). It is now clear that Bahrein was the centre of an important civilisation linking the sea-routes between Sumer and the Indus; that it was the source of very ancient mythological memories that were adopted by the Sumerians; that with its associations with fresh water and island immortality, it was a potent factor in the mass of legends that the writers of Genesis synthesized for their own purpose.

Too much to say that Adam and Eve walked there, of course—more's the pity. But Bahrein, I am personally convinced by the arguments, was the background to the Eden legend.

Only one snag, though. Hard though I looked, I never saw a single fig tree. . . .

May, 1971

5

The Night the Holy Mountain Erupted

THE TELEPHONE rang at 4.15. 4.15 in the morning. It was the extremely early morning of Tuesday, January 23, 1973. On the line was a friend from the Westmann Islands, the group of islands a few miles off the south coast of Iceland. And he was in particularly good form. A dentist to trade. In excellent form.

"Well," he said, "I've got rid of the wife and children. I've got the house to myself. The bar in the attic is well stocked. I've got my Leica handy. And now I'm enjoying a most remarkable sight. I'm watching the mountain on fire."

"Isn't it time you got to bed, old friend?"

"Bed? Are you out of your mind? I've got everything I need here, and you tell me to go to bed! Aren't you listening to the radio?"

"The radio doesn't start broadcasting until 7 o'clock in the morning. If you are hearing the radio as well as watching a mountain on fire, then it really is time you called it a night and went to bed."

"Just switch on the radio, and you may well hear something to your disadvantage."

And that was how the news reached me that a volcano had begun to erupt on Heimaey, the only inhabited island of the eighteen that make up the Westmann Islands. Some six thousand people had to be evacuated during the night. Helgafell, the "Holy Mountain," had erupted after lying dormant for 5,000 years, and the whole township was in direst peril.

And throughout the night, the whole population, men and women, young and old, forsook their prosperous homes and took to the sea in the 80 fishing boats which are the mainstay of the island's economy. The nightmare had become reality. The powderkeg on

which they lived had blown up. Their homes, their possessions, everything—everything had to be abandoned during that night of terror.

I managed to get there by ten o'clock in the morning, just as dawn was breaking (I begged a lift on one of the few aeroplanes that were allowed to land there that night—it's handy to have cousins and kinsmen about in emergencies). And I found myself a witness to the start of a new Pompeii.

The mountain behind the town had cracked in a great fissure nearly a mile long. The town itself was shielded by the mountain, for the fissure was on the far side. Throughout the length of this chasm, red-hot lava was spouting into the air. It was a classic fissure eruption of a kind only now found in Iceland. Not much lava-flow, but a constant bombardment of burning pumice and particles of tephra (volcanic ash).

People always tend to think that it is the lava that causes the damage. But they are wrong. Lava is limited. Even the greatest lava-flow on earth in historic times, which took place in Iceland in 1783, covered only (only!) 565 square kilometres. In a sparsely populated rural country, this causes little actual damage to buildings. The real damage is caused by the ash fall-out.

Within the first few days, only half a dozen houses in Heimaey had been burned down by splashes of lava and eventually smothered by lava flow. But another fifty had been wrecked by the weight of the volcanic ash spewed from the mountain.

This is what happened at Pompeii, too. It was the poisonous ash-fall that did the damage, not lava. For day after day, week after week, the rain of pumice, filling the streets, forcing its way in through doors and windows, piling up on roofs until the buildings collapsed under the weight, the rafters gave, the walls buckled and cracked. And the town drowned in tephra, ruined and irredeemable.

To see it happening before your very eyes is a terrible experience. What do you feel? Not the kind of therapeutic rage that a man-made bombardment induces, rage at the vileness of the act of destruction by other human beings. Not the solace of vengeance to come. Not even the kind of insulating fear for your life, for a volcanic eruption is only dangerous to life if you take the risk of going too close and getting hit by flying missiles.

No, there is a sense of awe, of helplessness, and of grudging admiration. Not dread, but awe: an awed respect for the appalling forces of Nature going berserk, of the fierce subterranean forge of the world cutting loose and breaking out. There is nothing to be done but to try to save what can be salvaged, and then wait patiently for the paroxysm to exhaust itself. It may take many weeks, many months, perhaps even one or two years.

Iceland is used to volcanoes. There is a volcanic eruption there on average once every five years, which makes Iceland just about the most volcanic country on earth. But somehow we had started to feel that we could cope. The disastrous eruptions of the Middle Ages, when Mount Hekla became notorious as one of the entrances to Hell itself, were things of the past; disaster relief organisations see to it that the widespread famine following on the destruction of farm pasturelands no longer happens. In 1783, a third of the population of Iceland died of starvation. That couldn't happen now.

But what had lulled Iceland into a false sense of security was that volcanic eruptions in the past have tended to happen far in the hinterland, or out at sea (the making of Surtsey ten years ago, for instance). The effect of these eruptions was indirect—windborne ash-fall would disrupt farm-life in whatever direction the wind took it, but not create a national catastrophe. The eruption in the Westmann Islands, in the only inhabited island, has brought home to the Icelanders for the first time the frightening possibility of volcanic activity in or around urban sites.

The devastation of Heimaey is a terrible blow to Iceland. This was the most important fishing centre in the whole country, supplying 20 percent of the fish exports on which Iceland depends so heavily. Where else can this capacity be found? Where is the fish to be processed for export—and this is right at the start of the rich cod season, remember.

Some 6,000 people made homeless and jobless may not sound much. But in the context of Iceland, with its population of only 200,000, it is equivalent in a UK context to the devastation of a city the size of Glasgow, with all that this would mean in terms of human tragedy and economic disaster.

And it has inevitably raised the question—could it happen to the capital, Reykjavik? Here lives almost half the country's population. Could a volcano start up on Reykjavik's doorstep? Is anyone or anywhere safe?

Geologists can make certain predictions, or at least extra-polations, about future volcanic activity. But Heimaey had been dormant for 5,000 years. Did anyone expect an eruption there? Does lightning strike twice after all, and thrice, and on and on?

So why live in the place at all? Why deliberately choose to set down roots in such volatile soil, in a country whose climate in winter makes communications difficult, in a country that may burst into flames any year, in a country where survival has always been difficult?

Ah, that's a hard question to answer. Why does the peasant continue to till the slopes of Mount Vesuvius? Why not up and settle somewhere less risky? Answer—because he was born there, and is attached to the land.

In Iceland, "attachment" has deeply-felt meanings. After centuries of struggling to survive, there is a sense of profound achievement, of having mastered Nature and matured into a nation in so doing. And the spring, when it comes, is so achingly welcome and beautiful. And the colours are so heart-breaking in their loveliness. And the air breathes an exhilaration of history and hope. And the lava landscape has taken on a serenity that only freshly-spent passion can endow.

A shared challenge, a shared fortitude, a shared knowledge of the difficulties and rewards of living here in Iceland—these are imponderables that other, older countries might well envy. They have to work twice as hard to earn their good living here in Iceland as in other places—but nobody cares.

To love one's country—not just the concept of "country" but the country itself, its mountains and lakes and glaciers—to love one's country with such innocent and joyful fervour as the Icelanders do! No volcano would ever be able to frighten them away. Even while the evacuation of Heimaey was under way, methodically and without panic, the talk was already of when the Westmann Islanders would be able to get back to repopulate the island.

Not, of course, that any Icelander (except myself) would admit to such romantic and sentimental notions. The Sagas, lovingly cherished down the centuries, have inculcated a dryness of style, a deliberateness of understatement, that eschews anything so wantonly emotional as letting your feelings show, or coming to the point too soon. A reporter on one of the national newspapers here

was alerted to the news in the Westmann Islands by a phone call just after two in the morning. It was his mother, an elderly widow.

"There's something rather serious happening here in the Westmann Islands," she said, and waited.

"Oh really?" her son replied. Pause. And when it seemed that no further information would be vouchsafed, his journalistic curiosity overcame the Saga reticence. "What's happened?" he said.

"An eruption has started on the eastern shoulder of Helgafell, near the Kirkjubaer farm. It began about two minutes ago."

They don't waste words in Iceland. They just get on with the job, as they have done for 1100 years now. And when disaster comes, they shrug it off, and buckle down to work again.

If there were tears, they all were shed in private.

February, 1973

6

How the People of Heimaey Brought
Life to the Ashes

I SUPPOSE you could call it an excavation, but not in the normal sense. Not in *any* normal sense. And it was just about the most moving scene I have ever witnessed.

It was on Heimaey (Home Island), the island township that was shattered in January when the Westmann Islands exploded in fire and volcanic fury. Spectacular and terrible as the eruption was, it was as nothing compared to the extraordinary exercise in human will and courage that is going on there now.

I was wandering across what had once been a street full of houses. A black, smoking desert of volcanic ash now, where in five hours of fateful wind-shift, the tephra spewing from the volcano had rained down on the town instead of drifting out to sea. There was grit in my shoes, dust in my eyes. Everywhere the evil reek of sulphur and brimstone. Somewhere deep beneath where I was walking, a row of houses had been buried, and were even now being cooked to death by the radiant heat from the molten lava nearby.

It was a scene of such desolation that my heart choked. All these houses represented the life-savings, the life-ambition, of young couples and old, families and friends. No one was killed, no one even injured, during the eruption, so swift and orderly was the evacuation of the 6,000 people who lived there. Compared with the terrible floods of Pakistan, say, or the earthquake destructions in many places in the globe, the death of Heimaey itself was a mere fleabite in the catalogue of human disaster.

No, it was not the scope or quality of the destruction that I was mourning. I grieved, of course, for those who had lost so much, who had seen their beloved island engulfed, day after inexorable day, by debris from the bowels of the earth. But it was something else that touched me almost to tears.

It was the fight-back.

Suddenly, in the middle of this blank sterile desert of black ash, a chasm opened before my feet. Or so it seemed, for I had been walking in a trance of thought. I looked down into it, expecting to see—anything. I don't know what. The jaws of hell, perhaps. I had been on Haemaey on the night of the eruption, when hellish fires burst from a great fissure across one end of the island, and when you have once seen into the cauldron of the earth, you never forget it.

No, what I saw was not death, but life. A group of youngsters were busy digging away with spades and shovels in the sunshine. They had cleared a long corridor into the mountain of ash on which I was standing.

They were excavating the churchyard.

I stood there stunned and bewildered. What an extraordinary thing to be doing! Here was half a town desperately needing salvage work, and these young people were digging out a cemetery! Let the dead bury their dead, I thought. What a waste of effort.

But it wasn't. Not by a long chalk. And gradually I came to appreciate that this was the most important work of all. This was the great act of faith that symbolised the Westmann Islands in 1973.

Every one of these young people was a volunteer. They had come from all over the world, on holiday to Iceland, carrying their rucksacks, thumbs at the ready to hitch a lift. And when they got to Iceland, they had heard of the rescue work going on in the Westmann Islands, and had volunteered to help. For nothing but their board and lodging.

Some genius it was who dreamed up the idea of directing their eager, generous young vigour to the churchyard. Let the bulldozers clear streets, let engineers fight to get the fish-processing plants to work again. Here was a totally selfless, totally symbolic act to undertake. And they did.

I met young men and women from Sweden, from Germany, from America, a girl from Shetland, who had gone to Iceland on spec for a job "away from it all," and had heard of the need for volunteers. She told me that they got a free flight to and from Heimaey from Reykjavik if they worked for six days, free bed and board (excellent board, she said), and £2 a day pocket-money. And a sense of deep satisfaction she could not possibly begin to articulate.

Some forty families have now returned to Heimaey to pick up the threads of their lives again. In the evenings, they come out to the excavation of the churchyard, and tell the young volunteers where to dig, how the paths of the cemetery lay, where they would find what stones.

And little by little the neat stones are emerging from the grim black ash. Head-stones that sparkle white in the sunshine. The smothered grass on the lairs is already turning a healthier colour. There are fresh flowers on the graves that have been uncovered. This is such an excavation as never was. Instead of finding only the insubstantial shadows of things long ago, like so many archaeological excavations, these youngsters are bringing the dead sharply to life again. About that scene there was an aching and beautiful sadness shot through with hope and aspiration.

And now I looked at Heimaey with new eyes. The miracle of Heimaey.

A little less than half of the houses have been destroyed under a new mountain of lava or smothered under the volcanic ash. The harbour, without which the island could not function, was direly threatened by the advancing wall of lava, but it stopped 60 feet short of blocking the navigation channel—and ironically improved it vastly, by creating a splendid new breakwater.

A million tons of volcanic ash have already been cleared away—and it's being put to good use. A lot of it will be exported, as valuable building and road-making material. Much of it has already been used to make much-needed improvements to the airfield. The rest is being dumped to smooth out hollows and dells in the rocky areas of the island, to make new houses to replace the old. The Westmann Islands had always been short of infill material. Now they've got as much as they can possibly want—and more.

There is now no doubt that Heimaey will one day be a going concern again. An opinion poll taken of all the evacuated Westmann Islanders revealed that only 10 per cent did not want to return to their former home island, because they had already settled into good jobs near relatives on the mainland. The rest will go back as and when the restored public services can handle them.

And that, remembering the holocaust of the eruption itself, is little short of a miracle.

And already, the Sagas are beginning to take shape. . . .

Take the way in which men battled against the volcano, for instance. In the 18th century, on a celebrated occasion, a priest prayed so hard and so passionately that the wall of lava that was advancing to engulf his church and congregation came to a halt. This time they used a more modern form of technology.

First they tried to create a new fissure in the side of the crater, to allow the lava to slide harmlessly into the sea. Six tons of TNT were applied. Compared with the force of the eruption, it had as much effect as a powder-puff. It was like setting a house-fly against a Jumbo Jet.

Then they hit on the splendid idea of trying to cool the outskirts of the lava to make it congeal into a barrier against the lava piling up behind it. After much trial and error, they began to get it right. Eventually, a million litres of seawater per minute were being pumped onto the molten lava, and by this means the scientists managed to deflect it from its course by some six degrees—enough to save a substantial part of the town, and the harbour channel.

This was man's first success in trying to control a volcanic eruption, and it opens tremendous new avenues for the future.

But there were other, less scientific, more human, successes, the very stuff that Sagas are made of.

There was an old woman called Sigrid. She had died shortly before the eruption, but in her lifetime she had been the bane of the authorities. She refused pointblank to pay taxes or rates. I own this house, she said. Here I am and here I stay, she said. The local mayor tried to argue with her, and got nowhere. The sheriff came from the mainland; but so stubborn and formidable was the old crone that he, too, gave up in despair. Then, a few weeks after her death, came the eruption. A huge wall of lava came sliding down the hill, mashing every house in its path. But when it reached Sigrid's house, unaccountably it veered to one side and left it untouched. Even the gods, it seemed, had hesitated to tangle with her wrathful shade. . . .

Tales of heroism and bravado are now being told. Of the man who, when he saw that his house was doomed, got out his camera, set it up on a tripod and a delayed-action release, and took a snap of himself and his family drinking champagne while his house was crunched to pieces behind him. That's giving destiny the two-finger sign, for you.

Then there was my kinsman, the geologist Sigurdur Thorarinsson, the foremost authority on vulcanology in the world. He had watched the progress of the eruption closely; he had predicted the course it would take, and that it would be over by the summer. Eventually, in June, the volcano started simmering down. The lava was still moving every now and again (it will take another thirty years to cool), but the crater seemed dormant.

Sigurdur announced, "According to my calculations, this volcano is now finished. And to prove it, I'm going down into the crater."

When people remonstrated with him, he replied that he had spent all his professional life advocating his particular theories about volcanic eruptions. If he went down into the crater now, and the volcano proved him wrong, he would rather die on the spot than live to see his life's-work in ruins.

So down he went, down a steel cable-ladder held by twelve strong men standing well back from the rim. They felt his steps twitching the rungs as he went down. Then nothing. Nothing for half an hour. In the old days, slaves who had attended their masters who descended into abysses to fight trolls would have fled by then, as Beowulf's companions fled during his fight with Grendel's mother.

But after half an hour, they felt the ladder jerk again. Step by step. Finally Dr Sigurdur Thorarinsson emerged, grimy and exhausted.

"The volcano on Heimaey," he said, without a trace of triumph, "is dead."

There will be a Saga out of it yet. But Heimaey itself is alive. Very much alive. And so is the churchyard. So are the dead. So is the past. And that's another, even greater, Saga.

September, 1973

Questionmaster and contenders for the 1977 *Mastermind* Final. The eventual winner, Sir David Hunt, is second from the right

7

I've Enjoyed Meeting the Quiz People

AH, THE QUIZ! With the finals of *Mastermind* looming up, the Quiz is much in my mind. How do they do it? Why do they do it? I confess I am mystified.

I myself have only appeared once on telly on a quiz programme, one called Quizball. I was supporting Kilmarnock (although Kilmarnock, in the event, would probably dispute that remark). It was a game, as avid viewers know, which was won by scoring goals by means of answering four, three, two, or one direct questions, in descending order of difficulty. Late in the game, with all to play for as they say, I was awarded a penalty or something, which enabled me to choose to have a one-shot question which, if correctly answered, would give us victory, for time was running out.

The question was, as I would have put it myself, a sitter. Name the American playwright who married Marilyn Monroe. Ha! *Death of a Salesman*! *The Crucible*! *A View from the Bridge*! Easy as falling off a log, might have been tailored for me. Take it easy now, son, take your time, the game depends on it, there's a breathless hush in the close tonight—all these thoughts flashed through my mind. This is the way that great players must feel at the moment of resolution, the "psychological moment," it used to be called.

All these thoughts flashed through my mind, as I say. The only thought that didn't flash through my mind was the actual name of the man who had written these familiar plays. Nothing. A blank. Imbecile vacuity.

The paralysis of mental processes was total, and seemed never-ending. Then, like a man slowly beginning to recover the power of muscular movement after a stroke, something started stirring in the

sludge to which my brain had been reduced. Torpidly, a name began
to form. It was not the name of the dramatist, but something like it.
My mother had had a kidney operation once, and the name of the
surgeon was Douglas something . . . Douglas . . . Douglas—
could it be Miller?

As my team-mates sat back contentedly, assured of a place in the
next round (who the devil could foul up a question like that?), and as
the question-master, David Vine, started harrying with his
eyebrows, I began fumbling for the answer.

"Douglas" . . . I said, hesitantly. "Douglas . . ." and here the
association started firming up . . . "Douglas . . . Arthur . . ."

At which point David Vine, who had no doubt already given me
more time than I should have had, stepped in like a sorrowful referee
stopping a one-sided fight.

"No," he said. "Not Douglas Arthur. It's Arthur Miller."

With that, Kilmarnock were out of the game.

And so was I.

I look back on that episode with mingled rage and shame. At my
own fearful inability to organise the teeming brain-cells into a
semblance of order when the chips were down. But I was left with a
deep sense of awe at the people who could, under pressure, scour the
recesses of their minds and dredge up half-forgotten facts when the
need arose—people like Bob Wilson the Arsenal goalkeeper, for
instance, and Jim Craig of Celtic, the dentist with the knack of
extracting information from his own head with a panache that left us
all gaping in admiration.

I was also left with a deep sense of compassion for the ones like
myself who knew the answers all right, but couldn't produce them at
the right time and so made asses of themselves.

So when the prospect of chairing the *Mastermind* quiz show came
up, I approached it somewhat warily. I looked it up in the dictionary
first:

Quiz: An odd-looking person or thing (Jane Austen). Well, you
might well say that, in the light of my experience.

Quiz: A practical joker; a hoax, a piece of banter or ridicule; a jest
or witticism. In my case, the jest or witticism was definitely on me.

The Oxford Dictionary goes on to give examples: "He's a droll
quiz and I rather like him mad"; "A true Quiz is imperturbable"
(1836). It wasn't until 1891 that the Americans, with their gift for

coining vivid slang words, started to use *quiz* in the sense we know it now: an oral examination of a student or class by a teacher, or as a verb to mean the same thing. And it is only recently that it has come to have the meaning noted in Chambers' dictionary: "a sportive catechism."

I like that. Yes, I like that. "A sportive catechism"—you'd think the definition had been made with Quizball specifically in mind. Especially when one of the obsolete meanings is "a yo-yo" (for that's what it feels like), and other is "a monocle with a handle attached" (cf. Himmler—"Ve haff vays of making you not remember").

As I sit there during *Mastermind*, rather pretentiously called the "Interrogator," I am uncomfortably aware of all these definitions, and all the dilemmas of the contestants. In the first place, I cannot for the life of me see why the contenders enter for it at all.

I can see the point of watching the programme, as people have been doing in gratifyingly large numbers: after all, it's the modern equivalent of the bear-pit or the cock-fight. There's a sadistic element in watching all sportive occasions, whether catechisms or not. On *Mastermind* this element is encouraged, I think, by putting the victim in a harshly lit black chair with all the accoutrements of menace and interrogation.

On the other hand, there must also be an element of masochism amongst the performers. They apply in their hordes for the dubious pleasure of being grilled in public, perhaps being humiliated (as I was, owing to my own inadequacies) if their minds aren't working freely, all for a tiny fee and the pleasure of being seen on television.

Given that, my admiration for the people who take part as contenders is unbounded. How on earth do they *know* so much? Where do they keep all that incredible assortment of useless or at least irrelevant information? And how on earth can they gear their brains to instant recall at the moment they require some scrap, some unconsidered trifle that was filed away years earlier?

How many islands are there in the Azores? What's the county town of Rutland? What's the largest freshwater lake in the world? Who did what, when, why, to whom, where? This endless string of questions, seemingly hopeless of answer, being smartly ripped off the line and flung right back. What's the currency unit of Thailand? How many Minoan palaces have been excavated in Crete? What is Ogam? What is futhark? How many of Henry VIII's wives were beheaded? Which English queen bore her husband the most children? What's the longest river in Russia? Who's the Marxist head of state in Chile? What dog achieved fame during the World Cup in England? What river is Black at both ends? (It's a trick—the Danube, which rises in the Black Forest and debouches into the Black Sea).

Some of the people on the programme have been particularly memorable, particularly the losers. There was the man who insisted on being described as a Redundant Tailor's Cutter (a good idea, that, because he got a host of offers of jobs and is now no longer redundant). There was the Welsh bus-driver, the Scottish pig-farmer, the Edinburgh dentist, the London greengrocer. All these had one thing in common—that systematic study was not part of their professional life, like the teachers and university lecturers and clergymen we have had on. The greengrocer who knew so much about modern French literature, the Burnley social worker who could specialise in both classical Greek theatre and the English legal system—people like these fill me with awe. But even more, the fact

that their general knowledge is so wide and so readily available—that's the real scrunch.

In *Mastermind*, interesting trends have emerged. One is that the specialist who chooses micro-biology or some such esoteric scientific subject will usually win his specialist round but will flounder in the general knowledge round, thereby perhaps confirming C. P. Snow's thesis of the Two Cultures. People who specialise in the humanities or arts usually do better in the second round, perhaps because their general reading is also likely to be relevant to the kind of prototype general knowledge question you find in quiz games.

The other is that people whose profession is study end up with an edge. The mind is trained to remember, and is constantly engaged in remembering, for that is the basis of our school examination system. Teachers have a built-in advantage.

The third fact, I think, is that there is a specific sub-division of humanity who are good at quizzes. Many of the *Mastermind* contestants have previously won the *Brain of Britain* contest, or done well in it. There seems to be a certain cast of mind which feeds on quizzes, which has nothing to do with intelligence as such, although intelligence is an obvious ingredient. It is a special kind of mentality which thrives on serendipity, the snapping-up of unconsidered trifles and the hoarding of them.

I must say, I enjoy *Mastermind*, as an exercise in refined ordeal. I've enjoyed having to bone up on subjects totally alien to me in the scientific field, as a measure of self-protection against the shame of not knowing whether the man's answer is right or not. I've enjoyed meeting this strange genus of homo sapiens, the quizman.

But most of all, I think, I have enjoyed an enchanting misprint that occurred in the *Belfast Telegraph* during a review of an early programme. It was reasonably flattering, or at least reasonably uncritical; but the compositor supplied the real comment when the title of the programme came out not as *Mastermind* but as "Masterwind."

Now that, it seemed to me, was getting priorities right!

December, 1972

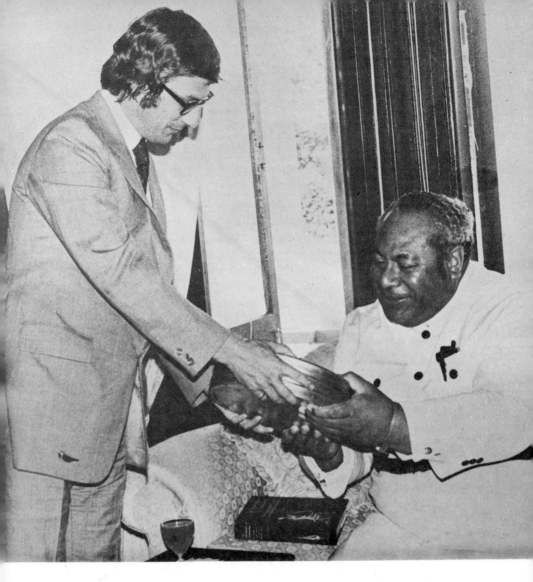

Colleague David Collison hands over a selection of BBC's *Match of the Day* to the King of Tonga

8

An Audience with the King
of Tonga

HIS MAJESTY King Taufaʻahau Tupou IV received us most graciously
in the Royal Palace on Tonga, a dignified, elegant wooden-built
house in a style that might be called Colonial Baroque. He looked
enormous as he sat there on the sofa awaiting us, as huge and
imposing as his unforgettable mother, Queen Salote.

"And tell us," he said, in a very quiet unemphatic voice, "what is
Bobby Charlton doing these days?"

So we told him, as best we could, what the great Bobby Charlton
was doing as manager of Preston North End. We told him how
Manchester United was faring in the struggle to stay in Division 1,
and we discussed who might win the next World Cup. When we
obsequiously suggested that Tonga might be in there with a shout,
His Majesty smiled but seemed unconvinced; because Tonga only
started playing football a couple of years ago, as the direct result of a
royal whim that decreed that rugby, the national sport, should be
superseded by football—and we had been advised by the High
Commissioner in London to take with us as a gift for His Majesty
three cans of filmed football games to please the new royal
enthusiasm.

The King explained that he thought football more of a team game
than rugby; that it could be played practically anywhere by small
boys with a round ball; that it was a game that girls could play, too;
and that it needed fewer players to make up a game than rugby did.
It all seemed eminently logical, apart from the fact that Tongans,
with their imposing physical size and strength, make natural rugby
players.

Still, it is one of the advantages of being practically an absolute monarch that one can indulge whims, or beliefs, of this nature on the spot. And that, most decidedly, is what His Majesty King Taufa'ahau Tupou IV is. Tonga is a self-governing kingdom, a British Protected State by virtue of a Treaty of Friendship ratified in 1901. All major policy decisions are made by the King-in-Council, and lesser ones by the cabinet of six Ministers, whom the king has the right to appoint or dismiss as he pleases (most of the present Ministers are of the royal family, anyway).

Parliament consists of the six Cabinet Ministers, seven representatives of the island's "nobles," or village chiefs, and seven representatives elected by the people. There are no political parties, and four of the present popular representatives are local lawyers. There are elections every three years.

It is not exactly what we would call a democracy. But it works for Tonga, because it is a natural development of the kind of social order which was operating when Captain Cook first stepped ashore here in 1773.

This social order was based on a pyramid of power and allegiance. At the top was the king. Owing direct allegiance to him were the various district or village "nobles," hereditary chieftains who in turn had virtually absolute power over their villagers, who were themselves divided into hereditary pecking orders. All the first fruits of the people's labour, spring and autumn, had to be presented to the nobles, who took their cut and handed them on to the king. The king thereupon redistributed these "gifts" to his own retainers, which freed them from the burden of growing or gathering their own food and allowed a degree of task specialisation at the top—stone-masons, craftsmen, even a royal undertaker. It was a fundamental form of early social organisation that made possible the making of large-scale monuments—and some scholars see it as a model for the kind of Stone Age societies that built Stonehenge and Silbury Hill and the great megalithic monuments of Brittany like the Standing Stones at Carnac.

The fascinating thing is that this social order is still operating in a recognisable form. We spent a week living in the little village of Mekave, on the northern-most island of the Tonga group, Vava'u. Here, the ceremonies, the dancing, the ingrained respect for the village elders and the village noble could still be seen at every turn.

We were greeted with a great *kava* ceremony, just as Captain Cook had been in 1773, two centuries ago. The village elders sat cross-legged on the ground in a wide circle on the turf outside the noble's house. At one end sat the noble, a gentle, dignified old man, incredibly small for a Tongan. On either side of him squatted his "talking chiefs" or heralds—two senior men who speak on the noble's behalf when he makes public proclamations, and who now roared out the responses of the ceremony.

At the other end, facing the noble, the *kava*-making was in full swing. *Kava* is the dried root of the *kava* bush, pounded in a mortar and mixed with water to produce a pleasant, tart-tasting drink which is said to have a slight narcotic effect on the nervous system. One by one, names were called out. Tongan ladies stepped into the circle to bear a coconut-cup of *kava* to each participant, who clapped his hands, once, to signify acceptance and drained the cup in one go.

Meanwhile, the gifts and first-fruits were brought into the circle—sugar-cane, *kava*-bushes, and the large pig which the BBC was thoughtfully providing. When the ceremony was over, the pig was despatched to the Governor of Vava'u, who in turn would theoretically despatch it to the king.

Pigs, we learned, were an indispensable part of the Tongan village feasts. Certainly, there were enough of them everywhere, rooting around and squealing. Occasionally, the morning stillness would be broken by agonised squalling and caterwauling as an unfortunate piglet was prepared for the night's feast.

All the food was cooked in an earth oven—a hole in the ground in which wood was burned to form charcoal. Food of various kinds was then placed on the smouldering charcoal, wrapped in coconut leaves—yams (root potatoes), breadfruit, fish, joints of pork, and so on. The food was then covered with leaves and earth, and left to bake for an hour. When the hour was up, the oven was opened, and the food loaded on to a stretcher of plaited coconut branches, and borne solemnly to table (well, there wasn't actually a table, we all had to sit cross-legged for hours on end, and I soon discovered to my chagrin that although my heart quickly became Tongan, my posterior and legs remained obstinately Icelandic, especially when the floor was concrete).

Our week in Mekave established the truth of two axioms about Tonga: that Captain Cook's designation of the Tonga islands as the

Friendly Islands held good to this day, 200 years later, and that Tonga is indeed the country "Where Time Begins." This is because Tonga is just to the west of the International Dateline and is the first country to greet the sun, 12 hours ahead of Europe. But Tonga is also the land "Where Time Begins" in that it retains so much of this magnificently pure early human society and culture. From it, and from its megalithic monuments (the structured tombs of rulers who died a thousand years ago, the mighty trilithons so reminiscent of Stonehenge), we can form a clear idea of the kind of early society that developed in Stone Age Europe.

But what will happen to Tonga in the future? Can these infinitely friendly islands withstand the pressure of modern times? Are villages like Mekave, with their relatively simple social structure, doomed?

Well, there are certain safeguards. No alien entrepreneur can come in and ruin the islands with "developments," as the French have ruined Tahiti and the Americans have ruined Samoa. All land in Tonga belongs to the Crown, and cannot be bought or sold. Every male Tongan on reaching the age of 16 is entitled to an allotment of eight acres and a house-site in a village, but he can also get work elsewhere—in the retail trade, or hotel-work, or the few copra plantations leased to resident Europeans.

On his allotment, he can earn about $200 dollars a year selling the produce of his coconut trees, and grow vegetables, yams, bananas, breadfruit, and so on. He can also grow paper mulberry trees, the bark of which is beaten by the womenfolk into a fabric called *tapa-cloth*.

It's not a very arduous job, running a plantation of that size. It is estimated that Tongans work an average of only two hours a day on their allotments, so one can see it as an essentially crofting economy—the allotment provides for a subsistence level of living at the worst. Visiting agricultural experts say that vanilla would be a much more lucrative crop, yielding more than $1,000 dollars an acre; on the other hand, vanilla takes a lot of care and trouble, and no return is forthcoming for the first two years, which doesn't suit the easygoing Tongans one little bit.

And is there any reason why it *should* suit them? Here we have some 70,000 infinitely friendly and charming islanders living in an idyllic world—a world in which no one can possibly starve, because of the richness of the natural vegetation. Anyone who is hungry can dig up some yams, pick some breadfruit, help himself to some coconuts. And that's the trouble, as the economists see it—there isn't enough incentive for people to toil to the toll of the factory bell. They can get along fine without too much hard labour. There is dancing to be done, *kava* sessions to be enjoyed, piglets to be consumed. . . .

But I guess it will change. Already, the old traditions are being forgotten, slowly but surely, as the older people die out. Already the advertising literature from America and Australia entices the young to harbour new consumer desires. Tourism is going to grow apace, as the world discovers this island paradise—and tourism cannot fail to undermine their culture, or at least commercialise it, which is probably the same thing. Tonga is no longer the isolated island Where Time Begins—regular air services from Fiji have seen to that.

All that I can hope for is that Tonga will resist more stoutly than the debilitated cultures of other South Sea islands have been able to do—and that whatever "progress" is achieved will be built on solidly Tongan traditions. Because I am convinced, now that I have visited several Polynesian islands which have already been overwhelmed by the crude materialism of more "advanced" nations, that we have more to learn from Tonga about the art of living than Tonga has to learn from us.

June, 1973

Professor Thom takes some of Stonehenge's vital statistics

9

The Men who drew Circles in Stone

WHILE THE REST OF France cringes beneath lowering clouds, this little corner of Southern Brittany—the Morbihan—basks in sunshine.

It is a place to enjoy, *par excellence* (you must excuse an occasional lapse into the vernacular—foreign travel gets me that way). What makes it even more enjoyable is to be travelling in the company of one of the most notable Francophiles and gastronomes of our day, that distinguished archaeologist Dr Glyn Daniel of Cambridge. For him, no journey, however short, is complete without a *dégustation* of a dozen oysters of the place and a half-bottle of the cheap and delicious local white wine, Muscadet; no village is complete without a small *crêpisserie* and its range of pancake specialities; no stop for coffee is complete without a mellow slug of the local applejack, Calvados. He has been coming here regularly for 40 years or so, and knows every restaurant and bistro; at his eager approach, menus primp and waiters wreath themselves in smiles. Sole meunière is the local delicacy, and lobsters, langoustines, stuffed clams, crab—anything that swims or floats, creeps or crawls, in the island-dotted Sea of Morbihan. And while he dégusts away with many a gesture and exclamation of delight, he talks enchantingly and learnedly of the archaeological phenomena that have brought more fame and fortune to Brittany even than the sun—the megalithic monuments.

Maturer readers will remember Glyn Daniel as the urbane and witty chairman of that former smash-hit archaeological panel game on television. *Animal, Vegetable, Mineral?* He is the foremost living authority in Britain on the Megalithic culture of Western

Europe—that extraordinary flowering of architectural and engineering genius amongst our Stone Age ancestors that reached its climax in Britain with the great Stone Circle of Stonehenge.

But Stonehenge was just the icing on the cake; up and down the west coast of Britain, and particularly in Scotland, are literally hundreds of these circles of standing stones, like the ones at Callanish on the island of Lewis.

Up to now, nobody has been quite sure what they were for, or even how old they were. The most one could say was that they must have served some inscrutable and ritualistic purpose, and the date was presumed to be somewhere between 2000 BC and 1500 BC. But now, for both these questions, modern science is coming to the aid of archaeology in the most unlikely way.

Take first the question of dating; and call to mind, if you will, a rather ugly, twisted, stunted tree in California called *pinus aristata*, the Bristle-cone pine. The only thing to be said in favour of this singularly ill-favoured tree is that it lives for an incredibly long time—5,000 years or so; and its age can be measured with remarkable precision by counting its tree-rings. This method of dating by tree-rings is called dendrochronology.

The value of this recent scientific aid is that it enables archaeologists to correct the manifest and puzzling inconsistencies that have become apparent in that other, earlier method of "absolute" dating, the Radio Carbon 14 test, which is based on measuring the rate of radiation loss in organic material from the moment it dies—wood, bone, antler, charcoal, etc. It has become clear that this rate was not constant, as had previously been supposed, and that there were considerable fluctuations.

Combining the two methods, it emerges that the Megalithic Age (literally, the Big Stone Age) lasted a great deal longer than anyone had suspected—from as far back as 4500 BC to 2000 BC or even 1000 BC; longer, indeed, than the Christian culture of Europe has lasted yet.

But what sort of a culture was it? Here another branch of modern technology is coming to our aid, in the pawky Scottish shape of Professor Alexander Thom, emeritus professor of Engineering Science from Oxford, now living in Dunlop, Ayrshire. Sandy Thom is not an archaeologist; he is an engineer. But for the past 30 years he has been spending all his spare time (and the spare time of his large and formidably talented family) making an accurate, scientific survey of the hundreds of Megalithic sites in Britain—many of them now so overgrown and damaged as to be hardly recognisable as such.

The result of all this labour is that Professor Thom is now convinced that the builders of the "circles" were highly accomplished mathematicians as well as engineers; they used a common unit of length, a "megalithic yard" of 2.72 ft, as well as megalithic feet and inches; and they understood and used the concept of Pythagorean triangles to create accurately laid-out ellipses, ovals, and flattened circles a thousand years and more before Pythagoras was born!

It sounds pretty incredible—to think that our remote forefathers were, in effect, Stone Age Einsteins with a passion for geometry for its own sake. But not only that; they were accomplished astonomers, too, and the circles and alignments were part of an elaborate, nationwide system for determining the calendar.

The implications are staggering; for the use of a "yardstick" throughout Britain suggests a sophisticated social organisation far in advance of anything so far suspected. And they may be more surprising yet; for Professor Thom has now come to Brittany, complete with family volunteers, tents, and lavish supplies of porridge oats, to see if the standard megalithic yard was in use on the Continent as well.

The sites that he is surveying here are very different from the ones in Scotland. They are not circles, but alignments—great sweeping avenues of standing stones, 5,500 of them in all: a breathtaking sight, these petrified battalions marching into the distance. The alignments of Carnac are assuredly the eighth wonder of the ancient world. But then, so is the Great Broken Stone (the *Grand Menhir Brisé*) at nearby Locmariaquer—a vast monolith that once stood as high as Cleopatra's Needle and weighed 330 tons; and so is the superbly decorated passage grave and chambered tomb on the island of Gavrinis (Goat Island) in the Bay of Morbihan—the Sistine Chapel of the Stone Age.

If Professor Thom really has found what he was looking for—a systematic use of the "British" megalithic yard—then clearly Britain and Brittany were closely associated all these thousands of years ago. It conjures up visions of a Stone Age Common Market that will give traditional archaeological thinking a resounding smack in the eye.

No one will be more pleased than Glyn Daniel—except, perhaps, Sandy Thom himself. Year by painstaking year, he has come to know these silent Stone Age forefathers of ours with a rare intimacy; every year his respect for them increases. He looks on them as fellow-scientists, fellow-Scotsmen—and therefore fellow-internationalists.

But what happened to them in the end? How did they lose the place? That's the biggest mystery of all. By the time the Celts of Brittany appear on the written pages of history, the Stone Age and its accomplishments were long forgotten. The bay in which Carnac lies quietly sunning itself was in all probability the bay in which Julius Caesar defeated the Venetii in a classic sea-battle in 56 BC, during his Conquest of Gaul prior to his invasion of England.

The Celtic tribes broke before the Roman onslaught, and took the sea-road to Britain, there to await another Roman assault and flee once more to the west—and back to Brittany. Thus does history repeat itself and come full circle.

I had not meant to squander so much of my space and your patience on the Stone Age. But I cannot resist the marvellous and slow unveiling of the past, the sudden shaft of light striking through the dusty dark of prehistory.

August, 1970

10

The Tale of a Tucson Tartaneer

I WANT YOU to meet Hughston McBain of McBain, from Tucson, Arizona. For he is a man after my own heart. He is a great original, and at the same time a great prototype. He is good value. He is everything one says to express delight and approval and enjoyment; because he is utterly, unself-consciously and totally self-consciously himself.

Hughston McBain of McBain, from Tucson, Arizona, is the Chief of Clan McBain. To prove it, he has a certification of matriculation from Lyon Court. He has three splendid eagle feathers in his splendid tartan glengarry. He has a McBain tartan kilt that aspires to be midi rather than knee-length. And he has all the instinctive sense of easy authority, of benevolence without condescension, of pride and fulfilment, that to my mind characterises the best of Highland Chiefs.

And he was over here recently, so I can't resist telling you about him.

Hughston McBain of McBain is an American classic. His father died when he was five years old. So in the time-honoured way, he put himself through school and then to university. At the University of Michigan he majored in journalism, and ran the University paper with two student colleagues destined to become famous in their respective fields: one was Chesser Campbell, who became the editor and publisher of the Chicago Tribune, the other was one Tom Dewey who ran and failed twice for President. The third member of the trio did all right for himself, too; because at the age of 39, which was real early for those days, he was appointed chief executive and president of one of the best-known multiple stores in America— Marshall Field & Co of Chicago, the Harrods of the USA.

The remarkable thing is that he did it from scratch. No vast family holdings in Marshall Field shares, no father or father-in-law to give him a pull or a push.

Straight after university, Hughston McBain of McBain

reluctantly decided that there simply wasn't enough money to be made in newspapers: not the kind of money he wanted to make, anyway. He decided that merchandising was the best bet; so he presented himself for an interview at Marshall Field's. Asked what he aspired to, he modestly replied that he hoped to prove good enough to make the grade as a foreign buyer, since he was interested in foreign parts and wanted to broaden his mind and his horizons.

The firm obligingly took him on and gave him a job in a department not even remotely connected with foreign buying—the claims adjustment department. His qualifications for this task, he concedes with engaging candour, were precisely nil. His function was to study complaints that were sent in, claims for compensation and that kind of thing, and deal with both the claim and the flaw in the organisation that provoked it. As a result, he gained far more real, first-hand experience of the workings of a great elaborate store than he would have gained anywhere else—as a counter-hand in haberdashery, for instance, where he could well have become a champion haberdasher but not an executive organiser.

And so, throughout his 20s and 30s, Hughston McBain of McBain moved inexorably up the ladder of promotion, reaching President by the time he was 39. He remained President for 20 years, and Chairman of the Board as well, before stepping down in favour of younger men ten years ago. He remained, and still remains, a director of Marshall Field; but in the meantime other directorates have come to him—the Illinois Bell Telephone Company, the First National Bank of Chicago, and perhaps most significant of all, Trans World Airlines. As a director of TWA, he has certain advantages of instant and inexpensive mobility that lesser mortals might envy.

He is now 69 years old. For a long time, he has been perhaps the most kenspeckle figure in Chicago, a pillar of the community, a brilliant and successful businessman in the great American mould. It is at this time in a man's life, when he's in his early fifties with a great and prosperous career mellowing behind him, that some tycoons get religion, or yacht-mania, or little girls, or something. Hughston McBain got clans instead.

His wife, who is Scottish, had unwittingly started it by asking him idly about his ancestry—the McBains are not the most renowned of the clans. And with that kind of enthusiastic affection for detail that abhors an ignorance, Hughston McBain started to try to find out about his genealogy. He wrote to various surviving members of the family, particularly aunts. He discovered that his great-great-grandfather had emigrated in 1811. He started to sketch in a family tree. It took him seven years of desultory enquiries, but by the end of these seven years he had a vast and proliferating family tree containing some 800 names, an enormous wallchart that spread, and spread, and spread.

He enlisted the aid of the Scots Ancestry Research Society in Edinburgh, who helped him push the roots of the tree further into the soil of the past by another two generations. Then he and his wife came over to Scotland for some first-hand research in the Inverness area, the traditional home of the McBains. He studied every churchyard in the area, making endless notes of McBain headstones. From Mackintosh of Mackintosh at Moy Hall he got a MS history of the Mackintoshes that included much unpublished material on the McBains. Gradually the formidable dossier thickened.

Hughston McBain discovered that there had not been a Chief of Clan McBain since the 1745. This saddened him. It did not feel right to him that his clan should not have a Chief. So he consulted other Chiefs. And he consulted Lord Lyon, when the holder of that august office was the inimitable Sir Thomas Innes of Learney.

Lyon growled agreement that a Chief would be a good thing; but there would require to be a direct blood relationship with the last known Chief. Hughston thereupon undertook to send Lyon all his researches in an effort to find the true Chief. (He says, and there is no reason to disbelieve him, that at that time he had no thought of becoming Chief himself).

It turned out from the charts that the proper Chief should be a certain Stewart McBain of Saskatchewan, a wheat farmer. Hughston wrote to him offering to support his claim to the Chiefship; but also thoughtfully provided some notes on the ancient Scots clan law of tanistry, whereby the Chief could nominate a successor from anywhere in the bloodline, and a ready-prepared document nominating him, Hughston McBain, should the Chief *de jure*, Stewart McBain, not wish to undertake the onerous responsibilities of the title.

There is no record whether any mention was made of any

sweetener, like a Jumbo Jet for Christmas (compliments of TWA), but Stewart McBain wrote back renouncing all interest in the Chiefship, and nominating Hughston with, one suspects, considerable relief, After due scrutiny by Lyon, this was all accepted, and in 1959, Hughston McBain became—Hughston McBain of McBain, 21st Hereditary Chief of Clan McBain (Motto—Touch not the Catt bot with ane Targe, or loosely paraphrased, If you aim to tangle with us cats, bring your shield).

But he was Chief only in name. Lyon had pointed out to him diplomatically that "we tend to look down our noses on Chiefs who own no land." So Hughston McBain of McBain set about getting some. But this turned out to be a lot harder than he expected.

In the Map Room of the Scottish National Library, he had discovered that the McBains had once owned about two miles of land above Loch Ness, near Dores. So he instructed a solicitor to try and buy about a hundred acres or so.

He was horrified to find that the Scots had no interest in selling land, especially to an American ("Why," he cried, "there aren't any real-estate brokers in Inverness, there's no work for them!"). After two long years, someone was reluctantly prepared to offer a measly two acres of useless heather hillside, for the price of £115. At first, McBain (as it is now proper to call him) refused in dudgeon; but his solicitor persuaded him to accept it, since other landowners were simply waiting to see what monstrosities he planned to develop there—a skyscraper, perhaps, or a drugstore no doubt. So McBain accepted, and in the end was glad of it; for as he admits, had he bought a hundred acres he would just have put a fence round them and forgotten all about them.

Instead, he set about converting his two-acre allotment in the hillside above Dores into a kind of heather Memorial Park for the Clan McBain at an overall cost of about £5,000, unassuming, with a memorial at the top commemorating the McBains of yesteryear, a couple of paths meandering up the heather slopes, a magnificent view down Loch Ness, and an air of quiet serenity and tranquillity.

It proved more popular than he expected, after he opened it in 1961. So popular, in fact, that with thousands of acres of heather to choose from, visitors unerringly descended on *his* two acres to dig up clumps of heather and cart them homewards in triumph. How to ensure the safety of his memorial heather? McBain, helped, he modestly admits, by a few glasses of whisky, sat down and composed a series of pleas in verse that would have turned McGonagall's heart to stone, then transferred them to little notices such as one finds in all parks exhorting you to Keep Off The Grass. These ones were of a much more refined nature, however:

> No burial ground
> No bodies around
> Just fond recollections
> Ancestor connections.

Or:

> A thief one day
> To our dismay
> Took plants away
> He'll rue the day

Or (this from the flowers themselves):

> We love it here
> Please let us stay
> We want to cheer you
> On your way.

My pen melts as it writes, as Sir Mortimer Wheeler once put it. Nevertheless, pilfering of heather from the McBain Memorial Park near Dores dropped by 90 per cent. Human nature is odd.

Every year, Hughston McBain of McBain comes back to Scotland. He attends the annual general meeting of the Standing Council of Scottish Chiefs. He goes to the royal garden party. Then he drives lickety-spit up to Inverness, to visit his beloved park and do a little weeding.

That's where I met him. And I found him totally convincing in this exotic role of American chief of a Scottish clan, totally absorbed in the serious business of providing a figurehead and focus for one of the smallest of all the clans, totally delighted by this unexpected new hobby to cheer his declining years.

Myself, I take my hat off to him.

August, 1971

Hughston McBain of McBain died in May, 1977. He has been succeeded as Chief of Clan McBain by his only son, James McBain, also of Tucson, Arizona.

11

'Please can we have our Past back?'

No, I cannot restrain myself. Like it or not, I'm going to tell you what happened on the last day of winter: Wednesday, April 21, 1971. Or call it the first day of summer. Whatever the season, the fact remains that in Copenhagen, a flag flew at half-mast over the Royal Library of Denmark—while in Iceland, a whole nation stopped work to welcome home three parcels of books.

I kid you not.

I only mention it, really, because it was an event that was almost totally ignored in our Press in Britain. Which is surprising. Because that remarkable and historic occasion could have far-reaching implications for other nations throughout the world.

Let me just tell you what happened. On the morning of April 21, the Danish frigate *Vaedderen* (literally, the Ram) came steaming into the bay of Reykjavik Harbour. There were 15,000 Icelanders cramming the quayside. And throughout the rest of Iceland, it was as if a plague had struck. No movement in the streets. Shops and schools closed. Silence. The whole nation of 200,000 was listening to the radio or watching a live TV transmission of the historic event taking place at Reykjavik harbour.

Just after the *Vaedderen* tied up, off came three members of the crew. Each of them carried a carefully wrapped package. These three packages had been locked in a cabin all the way across from Denmark to Iceland. Only the captain had had a key to that room; and twice a day he and an Icelandic representative had solemnly unlocked the door of the cabin to see if the "prisoners" were all right and the temperature and humidity to their liking.

They contained, these packages, two of the most valuable books in the world. They were the first instalment of some 2,000 ancient

books and writings that Denmark will give back to Iceland over the next 25 years. Because the Icelandic Sagas are coming home. And this gift by the Danish Government raises all sorts of interesting problems for other nations. Should countries like Britain and France and Germany now give back to their former colonies the art treasures they looted from them in the past, just as Denmark is now giving back the priceless Saga manuscripts removed while Iceland was a Danish colony?

Let's get back to the 21st of April. The parcels were snugly bestowed on the back seat of a black police car. Various dignitaries such as the Prime Minister made speeches of welcome at the quayside. Then the car was slowly driven through the streets of Reykjavik, past thousands of cheering people, to the University. It was like the Coronation in 1953.

And that afternoon, Mr Helge Larsen, the Danish Minister of Education, got up behind a battery of microphones, picked up the old leather-bound volumes, and said to his Icelandic counterpart: "There you are—Flateyjarbok. And Codex Regius."

Ah, magic names! (I know you think I'm nuts, so I might as well enjoy myself properly). Magic names indeed. "Flateyjarbok" means simply "the Book from Flat Island," and "Codex Regius" means "the King's Volume." So perhaps I had better explain.

Flateyjarbok is a great two-volume collection of classical Icelandic Sagas copied out on calf-skin vellum at the end of the 14th century on Flat Island. The scribes were two monks from the old monastery there, and the patron was a wealthy farmer who wanted to make a good addition to his library.

It was 450 pages long. That is to say, it had 225 leaves. And since they were big leaves, it meant that 113 complete calfskins were needed to make the book. The pens used were the quills of swans or ravens, and the ink was made by boiling the bear-berry plant to produce a black, glossy and extremely durable fluid. The margins were filled with "illuminations"—great flowery drawings and sketches, usually to decorate the initial letter of chapters.

Codex Regius is a very different matter. It is tiny in comparison: a mere eight inches by five in size, and 90 pages long. It was written a century earlier, round about 1270 AD, and it is considered to be Scandinavia's most valuable literary treasure, because it contains the *Edda*—the main, indeed the only source-work for Norse mythology and heroic legend that has survived. Without Codex Regius, Wagner wouldn't have been able to garble the story of the Nibelungs and the Twilight of the Gods into an endless opera.

The books are literally priceless. In the 1890s, the Americans wanted to put Flateyjarbok on display at the Chicago World Fair, because it contains the Saga accounts of the Viking discovery of North America 500 years before Columbus. They offered to send a battleship to fetch it, and to insure it for one million dollars, which was a lot of scratch in those days. But the offer was refused. Even battleships had been known to sink, and Flateyjarbok was irreplaceable. Not even a million dollars would be any consolation for such a loss.

So what were the Danes doing now, sending these marvellous books to Iceland?

Well, that's quite a long story in itself. The manuscripts originally left Iceland in the 17th and 18th centuries, when antiquarians became interested in the past. To the Icelanders, the old manuscripts were of no particular value because the Sagas were now being read in paper manuscripts, which were cheaper to make and easier to read. So they had no particular objection to the family heirlooms like Flateyjarbok and Codex Regius being taken to Denmark to the Royal Library—they had plenty of paper copies of them by then.

Then in the first decade of the 18th century, an Icelandic professor at Copenhagen University called Arni Magnusson (no, no relation) scoured the country collecting manuscripts and old papers. The Icelanders cheerfully gave or sold them to him. And he took them off to Denmark in 53 huge wooden chests (an unspecified number were sent off ahead on another ship, which unfortunately sank on the way).

Arni Magnusson housed his collection in Copenhagen. He was a real collecting maniac. He even married the ugliest but richest woman in Denmark to finance his further collecting. Then in 1728, fire swept Copenhagen. After several days, it reached Arni Magnusson's house, and about half the collection was destroyed.

In his will, Arni Magnusson left the remainder of his collection to a self-owning foundation, the Arnamagnaean Institute, with the responsibility of looking after the works and publishing them. This function it has carried out with great fidelity for 250 years.

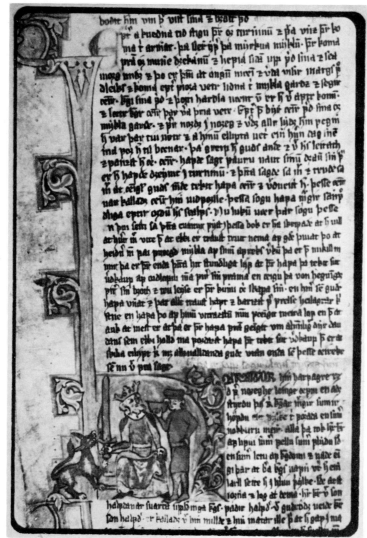

A page from Flateyjarbok

But to the Icelanders, as the movement towards independence began to burgeon in the 19th century, the manuscripts came to have a new significance, as something symbolic of their heritage as a nation. The Icelanders in their new-found national consciousness felt that the manuscripts should be in Reykjavik, not Copenhagen; and when Iceland eventually got her independence from Denmark in 1944, the only thing she asked from Denmark was the

Arnamagnaean collection and the choicest items that had been presented to the Royal Library.

It isn't the sort of request you can deal with overnight. After all, the Greeks have been asking for the Elgin Marbles back for umpteen years and they're no nearer to them now than when Lord Elgin stripped them from the Parthenon 170 years ago. In Denmark, successive Governments were reasonably sympathetic, but failed to get the necessary majorities until 1965, when Parliament at last approved the return of "Iceland's cultural possessions."

The Arnamagnaean, naturally, contested this decision with everything in its power. Lawsuit after lawsuit was raised, appeal after appeal was heard. Until finally, this spring, the only thing left to decide was whether any compensation would have to be paid to the Institute. It had already been decided that Parliament had not acted unconstitutionally; but the threat of compensation would

The manuscripts come home to Reykjavik

have killed the move just as effectively. In the original court cases it had been suggested, somewhat sardonically, that the 2,000 vellum manuscripts involved should be valued at £500 a page, based on the price of £36,000 which was fetched at Sotheby's in 1965 for a not very important 72-page 14th century codex. This would make the cost of the Arnamagnaean collection somewhere around £50 million, which would have stretched the generosity even of the Danes.

As soon as the Supreme Court ruled in March that there was no question of compensation having to be paid, the Danes got moving. As an earnest of the future, they parcelled up the two treasures from the Royal Library that they knew touched Iceland's emotions deepest—Flateyjarbok and Codex Regius—and shipped them off across the North Sea.

To understand the Icelandic attitude, you would have to assume that at the time of the Norman Conquest, the Normans had

removed to France not just the Bayeux Tapestry (which was needleworked at Canterbury) but also Stonehenge, The Anglo-Saxon Chronicle, *Beowulf,* the Sutton Hoo treasure (not then discovered, of course), and Canterbury Cathedral itself. And that owing to some brainstorm by Couve de Murville or President Pompidou, the French had just forced the Louvre to give them all back. Can you imagine it?

Of course you can imagine it. Just try to remember how we all felt when the Stone of Destiny was nicked from Westminster Abbey. Under all the tut-tutting, didn't we all feel secretly mighty pleased? Wasn't this a piece of Scottish nationhood coming back?

I don't suppose for one moment that the British Museum is now going to give back all its treasures to Egypt, and Greece, and Turkey, and Mesopotamia; or that the Louvre will do likewise. Museums are, by definition, acquisitive organisations, and would rather die than hand anything over (remember the row about whether the St Ninian's Isle silver should be allowed to stay where it belonged, in Shetland?). Museums even have this enshrined in law: nothing that passes in must ever come out. But this is manifestly silly nowadays, especially when most museums have got far too much on their hands already. The British Museum cellars and vaults are crammed with stuff that no one has looked at for years and years. We badly need a bit of fresh air in our museum thinking; we want to let things circulate more freely; and where nations or countries or even regions can now demonstrate that they can fully look after the objects which were taken from them in the past (no doubt to look after them the better), we ought to give serious consideration to the question of returning them and keeping replicas for our own use.

After all, replicas are just as satisfying to look at to all but the specialist; and the specialists can always get university grants to go and travel to the place of origin. They get that anyway already!

So spare a thought, as I suggest, to the momentous events of April 21, 1971. What happened on that day was more important than you realise; and in the long run, it could do everybody a lot of good. As for the Icelanders—I think they're still celebrating. In my own modest way I think I'm still celebrating myself.

June, 1971

12

Tutankhamun: Man and Mummy

IT WAS just like the old days again: the *real* old days, I mean, when journalists volleyed and thundered (on camels) down the Valley of the Kings in a nightly effort to get first to the one and only telegraph counter in Luxor; when *The Times* in all its ineffable smugness, comfortably clutching an exclusive contract, printed bijou accounts of the day's finds while all its rivals were reduced to inventing stories about the Curse of the Pharaoh's Tomb. And so on. Yes, those were the days.

And those days are upon us again. For in March, 1972 the British Museum puts on one of the great spectaculars of our time: the exhibition of the Treasure of Tutankhamun, discovered by Lord Carnaervon and Howard Carter away back in November, 1922.

Gad, it makes the pulses stir yet, he cried, reaching for his pith helmet and shouting for his mahoot. (Thinks: Is that a very large brown drink or a very small brown person?). For the Tutankhamun collection is unique: astonishingly, shatteringly, unbelievably unique. It is probably the greatest archaeological find of all time; and it's very hard to think it will ever be surpassed.

And yet, the tomb of Tutankhamun, which Carter stumbled upon intact, must have been relatively poor in terms of sheer bullion and wealth compared with the more elaborate tombs of the really great Pharaohs like Rameses II (the man who built the vast rock temples of Abu Simbel) or Amenophis the Magnificent. We have their splendid galleried sepulchres to this day, but they had been robbed of all their rich contents in antiquity. Compared to them, poor Tutankhamun's tomb is like a prefab—and *yet* it could provide tomb furnishings of such matchless artistry and craftsmanship. The mind boggles.

He was such a sad creature, Tutankhamun. (Incidentally, let's get the name right once and for all. It is built up of three elements, Tut-Ankh-Amun, meaning "Living Image of Amun," in which the Ankh, the cross-symbol you can buy as a life-charm, is the central element and Amun is the name of the chief god of the Theban pantheon, with the emphasis on the second syllable: Tut-ankh-am*u*n).

Not very much is known about him except that he came to the throne of Egypt about the year 1350 BC as a boy of 11, and that he reigned for only nine years. The man he succeeded was either his father or his father-in-law or his brother (or all three!), the man they called the Heretic Pharaoh—the strange, misshapen Akhenaten. Akhenaten was the son of that Amenophis the Magnificent. He was born Amenophis, Amenophis IV, named after his father, but changed his name to Akhenaten. And there you get one of these interesting quirks of dynastic history; for whereas Amenophis enjoyed great power and huge prosperity, the envy of the ancient world, his favourite son seemed to shun all that when he succeeded to the throne. He busied himself instead with religion and philosophy and art. So much so that he started a new religion, the worship of the sun-disc, the Aten (whence his name), and even tried to outlaw the former religion, the worship of Amun. He moved his capital from Thebes to a virgin site down-river at Amarna. He also married a woman who has come to represent the world's ideal of beauty far more than the Miss World competition will ever do: Nefertiti.

Between them they tried to start a new Egypt. Art in that period became strange and haunting, religion flourished in a natural and uninhibited way, the old priesthood was discredited: life was royal idyll. But in the meantime, while Akhenaten adored the sun in his new and remote capital, the great Egyptian Empire he had inherited began to crumble ominously as the young and passionate king neglected all the sterner disciplines of statecraft.

By the time Akhenaten died, after 17 years on the throne, his great religious and artistic reformation was under severe pressure as economic and military problems built up. The discredited priesthood of Amun made a comeback. Akhenaten's chosen heir, a young man (probably a son-in-law) called Smenkhkare, ruled only a few months; and after him came the puppet boy-king,

Tutankhamun. His name had originally been Tutankhaten, in honour of the Aten, but it was changed by the priests to honour the rehabilitated Amun. The actual rulers of Egypt began a systematic re-writing of history, of the kind familiar to us from Stalin's era. Akhenaten was reviled as "that criminal of Amarna," his sculptures and carvings defaced, his inscriptions all mutilated and erased: the king's name was simply wiped out with ruthless efficiency. The boy-king was weaned away from memory of the heretic.

Yet even so, he remained a suspect figure, and probably never entirely renounced Aten-worship. Some people think he was murdered in his late teens—certainly, his mummy is that of a young man of about 19. His golden face-masks, these incomparable portraits, depict him as a wonderfully handsome youth with more than a hint of tragedy lurking in his face. He cannot have had a very happy life.

But in death? There seems to have been something secret, even furtive, about the way Tutankhamun was buried; almost as if his private staff had reason to fear for the safety of the king in death.

For this was crucially important. In order to achieve immortality, the king's name and the king's body both had to be preserved, to stave off the onset of oblivion. His name had to be preserved by inscriptions in his sepulchre. And his body had to be preserved by mummification.

This was an interesting process. It took 70 days in all, and was basically a process of dehydration that took place in the aptly-named "House of Vitality."

First the internal organs were removed—the viscera and the brain, which would putrefy the most rapidly. The brain was withdrawn through the nostrils by puncturing the ethmoid bone. The viscera were removed through an opening in the left-hand side of the body. The abdominal cavity was then washed out with palm-wine and packed with linen impregnated with crushed myrrh and cinnamon and other aromatics. The organs were then treated in a dilute solution of natron and then packed in a special alabaster burial chest.

Meanwhile, the eye-sockets of the body were plugged with wads of linen, and the skull shaved. Then it was laid in a bed of dry natron to absorb all the residual moisture and dissolve the body-fats, leaving the skin supple. Then, after washing and treatment with fine ointments and resins and spices, it was wrapped in several hundred yards of fine linen bandages, to restore some of the shape and size lost through dehydration. Each finger and toe was bandaged separately, each limb (including the penis), and finally the whole body. A fortune in gold and precious jewels was tucked into the bandaging. Thereafter the whole lot was impregnated with unguents, oil and resin. In Tutankhamun's case, they put on too much resin, and all the tissues were badly burned and the bones themselves eroded.

And so the king's body was placed in its sepulchre, within a marvellous set of four decorated shrines and three golden coffins; and into the sepulchre was stuffed another unbelievable fortune in golden objects, the personal accoutrements needed in the afterworld. The doors of the shrines were bolted and sealed, one by one. The doors of the three chambers were bricked up, plastered, and sealed. The sloping passageway was filled with rubble. The outer doorway was bricked up, plastered, and sealed again. The steep stairway that had been hewn into the rock to make the sepulchre was filled in with rubble, and the entrance carefully concealed beneath loose stones and debris.

His staff must have heaved a sigh of relief. They had got the funeral over. Robbers managed to get in a little later, but they were disturbed before they had time to rifle the tomb, and the passage was filled up again and re-sealed—this time for good. And thus the king remained inviolate in his tomb until November, 1922, when modern archaeology caught up with him at last to offer him the posthumous indignities that all his greater predecessors had long since suffered.

I call it "modern archaeology." But that is a relative term; because the discovery and display of the Tutankhamun treasures is really obsolete in the minds of many modern archaeologists. The days of the Grand Discovery seem to be numbered—perhaps because the chances of a Grand Discovery are now so diminished. We are, in fact, looking back on another era: the era of the rich patron such as Lord Caernarvon (who went to Egypt for his health and developed an interest in digging) and the servant archaeologist like Howard Carter.

But fundamentally the difference is not one of personality—the idea that there aren't the giants of the past around any more. It is

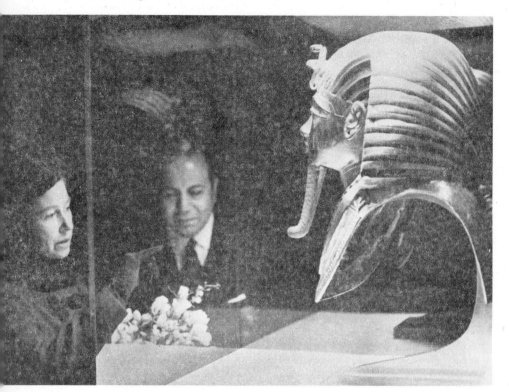

Queen meets Pharaoh—at the 1972 British Museum exhibition

strictly a real difference of approach. Because in the past most archaeologists tended to interpret their discoveries in terms of individuals—trying to rebuild the prehistoric past so that it fitted the mould of the conventional history book with its king lists and battles and so on.

In that context, the discovery of a *named* king like Tutankhamun was ten times as exciting as the discovery of an anonymous king. But the New Archaeology of today tends to concentrate not on individual men, but on man; not on events, but on processes; less personalised, but the result of human actions.

The New Archaeology is essentially science-based. It has grown out of the post-war scientific revolution, from which archaeology has benefited as much as any other discipline—with analytical techniques for determining the composition and age of artefacts, for instance, and hence their manufacturing processes and origin. But more recently a whole new batch of techniques has come in from cybernetics and geography, both concerned with data handling and classification in the field of numerous taxonomy; techniques of locational analysis: a whole new language too.

Archaeology, in fact, is trying to become a natural science, using the standards of the natural sciences, like setting up a hypothesis in order to test it. There is much talk of systems, of negative feedback, of multivariate explanations, of ethographic parallels, of the laws of culture process, of distribution patterns, interface relationships, and so on.

More and more, we will see the archaeologist wearing the white coat of the laboratory technician rather than the gumboots of the excavator. Or so it seems at present. The new generation of archaeologists are no longer satisfied with the handsome generalisations of the past, the sweeping vision of mankind's progress from barbarism to civilisation. It means that much of the romance of archaeology must perforce go out of the window, or at least the romanticism; but in the end there should be a much greater freedom of ideas and intellectual exploration.

We'll see. But meanwhile, no amount of analytical explanation or chemical feedback will ever equal the sheer physical excitement of seeing great and wonderful things that have been unearthed from the oblivion of the past. That's what the Tutankhamun Exhibition is about. And I don't believe we shall see its like again.

December, 1971

13

Lewis and Harris: how Utopia Came and Went

IT'S THE MIDDLE of a heatwave. It's the middle of a General Election. By the time you read this, both will be just a memory, pleasant or unpleasant according to taste and temper.

But right now, from where I'm sitting, there's no doubt at all which of the two is the more important. The heatwave, of course. Because I am writing this in the island of Lewis, in the Western Isles; and a heatwave in Lewis is something so startling, so magnificent, so unforgettable, that I would trade it for a dozen General Elections.

It's not, let me hasten to add, that Lewis never has good weather. Summer in the Western Isles can knock spots off the mainland—as it did in 1968, for instance, when London shivered in the rain and the islanders and holiday-makers sported glorious tans. But a heatwave here has a special, particular quality that's hard to match.

For one thing, it reveals a side of island life that too often gets ignored in the general libel of thick sweaters and gumboots. There

Lord Leverhulme made his Harris home here at Borve Lodge—and had this quaint walled garden built to his own design

are beaches here that put the Riviera to shame—I am thinking particularly of the Garry Sands at North Tolsta: a great long sweep of golden sand, not a pebble in sight, shelving gently to the sea, backed by sheltering dunes. If Lewis could guarantee a summer of four sunshiny months, the operators would be on to it in a flash; the grassy dunes would be buried under concrete and high-rise hotels; Blackpool would put the shutters up; no one would dream of Bermuda any more.

You see these sands in the heatwave, and you cannot imagine how it could ever have rained here before. You forget that to all intents and purposes, the winter only ended here a fortnight ago, and the rhododendron is hard put to it to keep a date with June. You forget the snow-flurries of April, the gales of February, the long dreich months of attrition.

You begin to realise why, with so many other places to choose from, the Lewisman grows so attached to his home. Every spring, his heart is taken by surprise. There is a physical exhilaration about the place that demands response: the hot, beating sun, always tempered by a mercy of breeze that makes sunburn lotion seem unnecessary until it is too late to soothe your wincing back.

It has its drawbacks, too. Take midges, for instance. The Western Isles breed a carnivorous species of midges that defy description and defence; I do believe they mate with clegs and mosquitos to add virility to the strain. They thrive on all the old and well-tried remedies—tobacco-smoke (that's merely an invitation to attack— there's no smoke without flesh), repellents, calomine lotion, paraffin. They *live* on the stuff.

The other day, rashly exploring a side road that petered out into a boggy track, my car got stuck. Not a midge was in sight. By the time I returned with help to extricate it, half an hour later, they were lying in ambush all around, more subtle than the Vietcong. No sooner did I bend my head to attach a rope to the underside near the radiator than—wham! They hit me with everything they had. I think I'd rather face a swarm of maddened bees than a single squadron of Lewis midges. Take refuge in the car—that was my only thought. It simply made things worse; for it merely brought a host of them into the car as well, and there I was well and truly trapped. They were able to eat me alive at their leisure.

Midges are the denizens of peat bogs. And I for one would be loath to see Lewis without its peat bogs. There's a million acres of the stuff in Lewis; and right now, in the peak of the peat-cutting season, what an extraordinary sight it is to see the land being sliced and trenched on every side, the peat getting blacker and better the further down you go. Useless stuff, you might think, looking at these vast expanses of brown and green wastelands. And yet, in three days of hard toil, a man can win himself enough fuel to last him all winter. How much of *your* time goes in earning enough to pay your heating bills?

There's another thing about Lewis you'll find in very few places on the mainland now. Hospitality. It's never too late for a cup of tea and heaped plates of baking and sandwiches, never too early for a genial dram. I have never known a people to whom hospitality comes so easily; it is second nature. And not just the hospitality of the table and the sideboard: the hospitality of time, and patience, and infinite courtesy.

My business here in Lewis is to make a film about one of the most fascinating episodes in recent island history—the time, just after the First World War, when the first Lord Leverhulme bought the islands of Lewis and Harris and tried to turn them into a Utopia of

Lord Leverhulme—a flamboyant figure in the life of the Long Island—flanked by Harry Lauder and Provost Roderick Smith of Stornoway

modern progress. He was going to introduce modern industries based on island resources—fish in particular, but also peat (for electricity), wool for tweeds, willow for basket-making, fruit for jam-making, flax for whatever you do with flax. He was going to build a railway, build modern harbours, build fish-canning and fish processing plants, build a huge fishing fleet.

Well, he failed. He withdrew from Lewis after spending £1,500,000 of the £5,000,000 he had originally earmarked. He was defeated by a combination of the world economic slump in the early twenties and a conflict of values.

What fascinates me about it is that here was the quintessential clash that no sociologist has ever been able to solve: the clash between a progressive "reformer" and an ancient, traditional culture. Leverhulme might have succeeded if he hadn't been determined to stamp out crofting in the islands, because to his business mind it was a wasteful and incompetent way of life. He tried to quantify crofting as a way of life that produced only eight shillings a week, compared with the £3 a week that men could earn in his fish factories.

But who can quantify the indefinable quality of crofting? The indefinable qualities which crofting enshrined? Who is to tell a crofter that he is wasting his life? That £3 a week in a council house is better, or more valuable, or more virtuous, than eight shillings a week in a croft-house? Today it is generally recognised that crofting is an anachronism that can hardly be expected to survive as new generations prefer newer ways of life. But that is simply a matter of preference, not of economic arguments. Crofting is unrealistic. Crofting is the economist's nightmare. But crofting is—was— crofting; and it nurtured generations of fine men and women who were quite content to live in sub-standard houses and send their sons and daughters to universities and armies and settlements abroad.

Leverhulme could not fully understand the depth of this attachment of the Lewisman to his croft. No one in Lewis had any objection to his industrial schemes—quite the opposite. Everyone in Lewis, crofters and townspeople alike, welcomed them with open arms. But the crofters couldn't see why they couldn't be carried out side by side with their own traditional way of life. Leverhulme, for his part, feared that crofting would sap the industrial discipline required for a plant to function efficiently. His shrewd business mind couldn't understand why his island piper was prepared to be sacked for taking a week off to see to the potatoes on his croft, when his wages at the castle could have bought him ten years' supply of potatoes instead. You can't run a business or a factory if all the workers rush off every spring and autumn for weeks at a time to tend to their crofts, or when the fishermen refuse to catch fish just because it happens to be Sunday.

So Leverhulme made crofting an issue. And when there was opposition from the crofters, when the crofters were obstructive the way a chicken is obstructive when you try to wring its neck, Leverhulme withdrew.

Some said he used the opposition from a handful of crofters as an excuse to withdraw because he himself was running short of money. Some said he withdrew in a huff because he hadn't got his own way—and the founder of the Unilever empire was a man very used to getting his own way. Some say he withdrew because he saw it was hopeless even to try to make Lewis a going, viable proposition in terms of modern industry.

Legend tends to read the story as the benevolent philanthropist defeated by a bunch of workshy Stone Age peasants who couldn't see on which side their bread was buttered; that Lewis refused to be dragged into the 20th century; that it's been paying the penalty ever since, in depopulation and unemployment

Well, there's no easy answer. Today in Lewis, people remember the Leverhulme episode with real regret as an opportunity missed—but who did the missing? They recall Leverhulme with affection as a man who was trying to do what he thought best. They are understandably resentful of the imputation that their fathers threw Leverhulme out because he wanted to persuade them to do an honest day's work—for this is a gross misinterpretation. The failure of the Leverhulme dream was a combination of many factors—political intransigence by the Scottish Office, personal intransigence by Leverhulme himself, and the intransigence of land-hungry ex-servicemen wanting the land they had been promised before the war, the homes for heroes they had fought for.

Today the Crofters Commission tries to merge and expand the little, non-viable crofts into farms. The Highland Development Board tries to encourage the very industries Leverhulme had tried to establish. The Scottish Office spends money on roads and construction projects that Leverhulme had been prepared to finance out of his own pocket. That's the real irony of the failure.

All that was 50 years ago. In 50 years' time, what then? In 50 *days'* time, after all, the heatwave may or may not be over; England may or may not have retained the World Cup; Labour may or may not have won the Election. And none of this matters so much as Lewis itself does, this island of quiet and dignified tradition, of a culture older than any of ours, this island of hospitality and sanity in the sun. In the inevitable process of time and change, will Lewis be able to retain its special flavour, its special sense of values?

I would dearly like to think so; for I feel a special attachment for this place, a blend of nostalgia and sentiment and envy: nostalgia for a lost innocence, sentiment informed by a thousand friendships, envy for a way of life that would not suit me personally but whose virtues I can well discern. The Norse name for Lewis was, literally, "Song-Houses," and I cannot imagine a name more apt. Lewis *is* a song: a song of innocence and exile, of summer and winter, of crotal and white. Its grace-notes are a flourish of gaiety on the underlying melancholy theme, the pentatonic dirge of Gaeldom fighting its battle for survival in a world careless of its qualities.

Perhaps Gaeldom is an anachronism in this day and age. Perhaps crofting is an anachronism. Perhaps islands themselves are anachronisms, too. But if they are, and if they ever become extinct, how much the poorer we shall be, and how much we shall regret their passing.

But what sort of talk is this? I'm sitting in a heatwave in Lewis, and should be counting my blessings, not mourning the unborn future. Tomorrow is another day—and all too probably, it will be.

July, 1970

14

Have you Heard the One about the Barometer and the Skyscraper?

LET ME TELL you a story I heard on my travels. A splendid, moral, parable of a tale, eminently suited to this season of school sessions starting and bleary-eyed children snailing to school on unusually shiny feet.

It comes from Denmark, where it was published in the *Engineers' Weekly,* of all things. And it concerns a certain question in a certain examination in physics.

The question on the exam paper read: "Describe how to determine the height of a skyscraper with a barometer."

One student answered as follows: "You tie a long piece of string to the neck of the barometer, and then lower the barometer from the roof of the skyscraper to the ground. Thereafter the barometer should be pulled up again and the string measured, and the length of the string equals the height of the skyscraper."

The teacher gave the student no marks at all for this answer, but the student demanded full marks—10 out of 10—on the ground that the answer was indisputably correct; and he went on to argue that conventional educational systems were positively injurious to students. He appealed to the university authorities, and eventually it was agreed to call in an impartial arbiter to decide the issue. The choice fell on an American teacher of science at the University of Washington, called Alexander Calandra.

Dr Calandra pointed out that the student deserved full marks from one point of view, in that he had answered the question correctly and satisfactorily. On the other hand, to give him full marks would suggest that he had displayed an acceptable knowledge of *physics*, which his answer in fact had signally failed to reveal. So Dr Calandra suggested that the student be given a second chance to answer the question, and this was agreed.

The student was given six minutes in which to answer, and was told that the answer would have to show some knowledge of physics. There was complete silence for five minutes. The student sat there, frowning heavily, deep in thought, but uttered not a word.

When there was only a minute left of the allotted six, Dr Calandra asked the student if he had given up. He replied that he had several answers to the question, and was merely deciding which of them was the best. Then he said.

"You take the barometer up to the roof of the skyscraper, drop it over the edge, and measure the time it takes to reach the ground with a stopwatch. The height of the building can then be worked out in terms of the formula h=½gt² (height equals half times gravity-time, squared)."

Dr Calandra awarded the student nine out of ten, and both the student and the teacher accepted this arbitration. Afterwards, however, Dr Calandra asked the student in private what he had meant when he said he had many answers to the question to choose between.

"Well," said the student, "you can measure the height of the skyscraper in several ways. If the sun were shining, for instance, one could measure the length of the barometer, then set it up on end and measure the length of its shadow. Then you measure the length of the shadow of the skyscraper, and thereafter it is a simple matter of proportional arithmetic to work out the height of the skyscraper."

"What about the other methods?"

"Yes, well, then there's a very ordinary and commonplace method, whereby you simply walk up the outside emergency staircase with the barometer, and mark off its length with a pencil on the wall of the skyscraper. Then you just count up the pencil marks, and work out the height of the skyscraper in barometer-lengths. That's really a very simple method.

"And then of course there is also a highly scientific method, whereby you tie a short piece of string to the neck of the barometer and swing it like a pendulum, first at ground level and then on the roof of the skyscraper, and then work out the height of the building by the difference in the gravitational restoring force (T=2π square root of *d* over *g*).

"And there are several other possible methods. The easiest and no doubt the safest method is to knock on the door of the janitor, and when he opens the door, say to him, 'Sir, if you would tell me how high this skyscraper is, you may have this handsome new barometer'."

At this point, Dr Calandra weakly begged the student to say no more, but asked him if he really didn't know what the correct, orthodox answer to the question was? "Of course," he replied scornfully, "but all through school and university the teachers kept telling me to exercise independence of mind and apply scientific methods, and that's precisely what I decided to do. . . ."

I found the story of this defiant student enchanting, and morally uplifting. Only one thing bugged me, however—and that was the *real* answer to the question. In a technical journal like the *Engineers' Weekly,* it was no doubt considered unnecessary to print anything so self-evident. It has taken me ages and ages to find out, but at last a co-pilot on a plane I was on recently cleared it up for me, on the analogy of how an altimeter in an aeroplane works. An aneroid barometer simply measures the air-pressure, and by noting the difference in air-pressure at ground level and on the roof of the skyscraper one can work out the difference in height. Thus, standard air pressure on the ground is 29.92 inches, or 1,013.2 millibars. Now say the pressure on the roof of the skyscraper was 1,000 millibars, the difference of 13.2 millibars would be equivalent to a height of 364 feet. Ergo, the height of the skyscraper is 364 feet, or so he said, anyway.

Independence of mind. Scientific methods. Is that really what our teachers tried to drum into us? Going through the garage the other day, I began to doubt it.

"Going through the garage" is an annual festival. It means the time is coming when the garage doors will have to be shut against the winter weather, and that means clearing the spring and summer debris that has gradually silted up the far end so that the car can only get halfway in.

And it's usually the *same* debris, what's more—the stuff that gets summarily turfed out of my study in a Herculean spring-clean, and then gets reinstated in the autumn because I can't bear to throw it all out.

It's my schooldays, you see.

Mouldering cardboard boxes, crammed with junk, the bric-a-brac of times past. Every year I'm going to consign them to the bonfire; but every year I relent.

Out comes a crumpled blue file, damp round the edges, soggy with neglect and reproach. In portentous capital letters, SHORT STORIES, DRAFTS AND FINAL.

There is a coating of rust on the paper where the paperclip had clenched the paper together. Some of them were stuck to one another. All thoughts of autumn cleaning are forgotten, and the afternoon passes in a trance of dusty hands and wondering memories. Did I really write that? Could I conceivably have set these words to paper? And then you remember . . . remember the evenings, late late at night, desperately pen-chewing, dreaming dreams of literary greatness but not daring to show the work to anyone in case the dream were shattered.

Independence of mind? Even at this remove, I can tell at a glance which author I had just been reading. Ah yes, that was Hemingway—Maugham—Virginia Woolf—James Joyce—that American writer, what was his name, yes, William Faulkner (never a comma or a full stop all paragraph)—Angus Wilson. Independence of mind, my foot.

And what about all these crammed notebooks? MILTON: "Approach must be aesthetic as well as historical. Note aesthetic parallel in 'Absent thee from felicity awhile' and 'Repayreth home from wordly vanity'; but the contextual associations are much greater in Shakespeare's lines than Chaucer's. . . ."

I haven't the faintest idea, today, what that means.

SWIFT: "There is an interval of approx 30 years between the writing of *The Tale of a Tub* and *Gulliver's Travels.* Between these crucial publications we can find a wealth of pamphleteering material and verses, satirical political writing and some extremely interesting and illuminating correspondence"—(Bet I never read the correspondence itself—just what someone had written about it). "By assuming disguises he gave full rein to all his powers, both as dramatist and novelist. He found the right vantage point from which to observe, and thus proportion and clarity is gained. His work gains fullness and variety. . . ."

There it all is, every banal, threadbare sentence, on neat lined school-paper. From which critic had these thoughts been plundered?

"The imagination has two focal points, one fixed, the other always advancing. In Homer's Odyssey, the two foci come together: the imagination strikes to the spirit of adventure, and the desire to know." Presumably, when I wrote that as a preamble to an essay on *The Ancient Mariner,* I actually meant something—it's so earnest, so meaningless, it must have meant something. Perhaps I was trying to apply scientific methods of criticism, but I doubt it.

To the bonfire with it! I cry. No, hang on a minute, here's an envelope of exam papers. Fancy keeping exam papers!

Write a composition not exceeding three foolscap pages in length on one of the following subjects:

(a) Social Security in Post-war Britain.
(b) Describe as vividly as you can any impressive ceremony you have witnessed.
(c) We are becoming more and more a nation of town and city dwellers: discuss the effects, good and bad, of this development.
(d) "One crowded hour of glorious life/Is worth an age without a name." "Give me a quiet life." Write on "The life that appeals to me."
(e) Shadows.

That was the Senior Leaving Certificate, 1945, Terminal Examination in English. I cannot remember ever having seen that paper. But I had marked it with my name (I marked *everything* with my name in those days), and put a little tick against (e). So I wrote about Shadows, did I.

I wonder what I wrote?

I went through every exam paper, that afternoon. Not a question could I have answered today. Greek, Latin, mathematics—all one, like the shadows. Still I ploughed on, looking for something. But I never found it. I was looking for a question which started, "Describe how to determine the height of a skyscraper with a barometer. . . ."

October, 1972

15

No Passport in the Home
of Freedom

IT'S EASY to go off people. By King George, you can go off people!
(The Greek Colonels, I mean).

There I was at Athens Airport, looking forward to a quiet kip on
the direct flight back to London to make up for the gala farewell
dinner the night before, when I discovered to my growing dismay
that the filing shambles I call my briefcase did not appear to contain
my passport in any of its voluminous folds.

There was nothing to do except advance boldly to the barrier and
inform the boot-faced policeman there that I had no passport on me,
but wads of identification papers which would do just as well. The
boot-face became even bootier-faced. I was informed that without a
passport I could not leave the country, and that until I managed to
achieve one, I would perforce be required to remain in said country.
End of first conversation.

I had a pretty fair idea where the passport was. Greece is one of
those places where your passport is removed by the hotel
receptionist and given back to you when you leave. Mine had not
been given back to me when I left, because I had forgotten to ask for
it (I am always in some haste when leaving hotels for a morning
plane). But there was no time to have it fetched out to the airport
before the plane left. Ergo, I would stay. End of second
conversation.

But under international law, I argued (without much confidence),
a passport is not required to *leave* a country. It may be required to
enter a country, but it was simply an accepted and acceptable means
of identification. And I was sure, I said (with even less confidence)

that Colonel Papadopoulos would be happy to accept this interpretation if someone would take the trouble to telephone his office. There was no reply at all to this. It was treated with the disdain it no doubt deserved. End of third conversation.

One more try. With a show of simulated righteous indignation (there were only four minutes left before boarding) I demanded to see the Icelandic Ambassador. There is unfortunately no Icelandic Ambassador in Athens, but I didn't suppose that the British Embassy would be anything other than politely amused at my predicament, and would undoubtedly disclaim all responsibility. However, the implied threat of all-out war between Iceland and Greece over my missing passport (a fifty-mile limit for passport-losing, perhaps?) made singularly little impression. End of fourth conversation.

Well, I suppose there are worst places in which to have to kick your heels all day than Athens International Airport, although it has not been my misfortune to encounter them. BEA did its usual splendid job to get me on a later plane, and as the hours passed my wrath began to diminish. After all, it had been my own damned silly fault, etc. One couldn't blame the colonels for strict adherence to the book, etc. The way you are treated by American Immigration authorities (even when you are only in transit through the place) makes the Greek police state feel like a haven of democratic tolerance, etc. Perhaps if I had tried to bribe them with the last of my drachmae, etc.

Anyway, I got out safely in the end. Broken schedules were repaired. I think that what fundamentally irritated me was the contrast between Greece's manifest desire to create a good image to the world at large, and this high-handed refusal to make any conciliatory move towards a traveller in difficulties.

As I said, it makes you go off people a bit. But not off Greece. Greece will always remain one of the most enchanting countries I know, and I mean the word in its fullest sense. "Enchantment" is the word that keeps springing to mind, and indeed much of Greek history is about enchantment. I'm thinking of Odysseus tying himself to the mast in order to be able to savour the enchantment of the Sirens without the terrible aftermath of yielding to it. I'm thinking of the hundreds of European Philhellenes from Byron downwards or sideways who felt that enchantment early last

Magnus and Sir Mortimer land on Delos, May 1972

century, and poured their dreams and often their blood into the Greek struggle for independence against the Turks.

I've been reading a splendid book about that period: *That Greece Might Still Be Free–The Philhellenes in the War of Independence,* by William St. Clair (Oxford University Press, £5). Nothing seized the imagination of European idealists to the same extent until the Spanish Civil War in the 1930s. In their hundreds, the dreamers and the adventurers, the remittance men and the eccentrics, the imperialists and the missionaries, the mercenaries and the speculators—they all flocked to Greece during that vicious decade in the 1820s, when the Greeks fought for their freedom as desperately as they fought after the Second World War.

For the romantics like Lord Byron, it was a case of trying to recreate the lost, echoing glory of Athens in the time of Pericles. Now there was a man! The Churchill of his age. And like all great statesmen, unscrupulous to boot. I'm thinking here of the most famous of all the monuments of classical antiquity—the Parthenon of Athens. It was built in the 6th century BC at a time, as Sir Mortimer Wheeler has put it, when the man, the moment, the mood and the means all came together at the right time.

The man was Pericles: a dazzling political figure, inheritor of and creator of a new Athenian mood that had been born away back in the days of Marathon, when 5,000 Athenians and a handful of allies from Plataea threw back the Persian host of God knows how many thousands at a cost of only 192 dead (their great burial mound is one of the most moving sights in Greece). The Persians had come back and had devastated Greece and Athens in particular, and the Greeks had decided to leave the shattered temples on the Acropolis as a permanent memorial of hatred.

But a generation later, the Athenians were tired of listening to their elders' war stories, and felt a new sense of strength of their own. They had founded a confederacy of allies, with its

headquarters at the tiny island of Delos. This Delian League was financed by all the allies, but as time went on and the Treasury grew and no enemies appeared, it began to seem as if all that money lying in Delos could be put to better purpose.

Or so it seemed to Pericles.

Thus the man, the mood, and the moment were right. And lo and behold, there in Delos lay the means.

So Pericles argued that the money could best be used building a splendid memorial to Greek brilliance on the Acropolis, that sacred place. He had at his disposal a school of brilliant sculptors under Pheidias. And had not the Athenians suffered worse than any other city state in Greece?

And so the Parthenon was financed at colossal expense. And it rose from the burnt limestone pedestal of the old temple (you can still see the cracked and discoloured stone course almost at ground level) to become one of the great architectural masterpieces of the world. Every straight line you see is subtly curved, to correct the natural optical distortion of the human eye. If the vertical axes of the pillars were continued upwards, they would meet at one mile overhead. And so on.

The sculptures that adorned it were created by Pheidias and executed by his pupils. Some are superb, others less inspired. For instance, in the splendid little museum on the Acropolis, you can see how some of the horses in the frieze (the "Elgin Marbles") have manes which are simply depicted as perfunctory scratches; others, done by a master hand, suggest all that marvellously fluid movement that Greek drapery in statuary has at its best.

Pheidas' proudest achievement was an immense statue of Athene in the inner chamber of the Parthenon. Eventually that was removed to Constantinople, where it was destroyed in the 6th century AD or so. But the Parthenon, brain-child of Pericles, midwived by Pheidias, financed unwillingly by the Delian League, remained.

Over the centuries it began to moulder away. It suffered awful destruction under the Turks, when it was used as a powder magazine and was blown up by a lucky Venetian artillery shot.

Then came Lord Elgin, and his salvaging of the remaining sculptures left on the Parthenon. I always find it hard to think straight about Elgin. In one respect, it was sheer looting: in another, it was a noble and selfless act of rescue. One has only to look at the few sad pieces left on the Parthenon today, worn and eroded by air pollution, to realise that if Elgin had not removed them when he did, they would not have been worth looking at today, much less removing. His motives were complex, on the one hand inspired by a real love of classical art and a desire to save it for Europe and the world, on the other by a less worthy desire to stop the French getting their hands on the stuff.

Anyway, he paid dearly for his trouble. The cost ruined him financially and made his later life a misery. And it was one of the foremost Philhellenes, Lord Byron himself, who caused him the most bitter distress, turning public opinion against him by some savage and biting satirical verses about his collection.

That, I suppose, was the mood of the time. Byron threw himself heart and soul into the Greek cause. When Elgin had been busy on the Acropolis, the Greeks had been under Turkish rule, and to Byron the removal of this heritage became a symbol of their subjection and humiliation. Pericles would never have stood for it.

Aha! We are back with Pericles. What really was the freedom that Pericles stood for? What really was Athenian democracy? Did it

The Dog by Phaidimos at the Acropolis Museum

(and I ask this diffidently) include the right to travel unimpeded even if you didn't have your damned passport with you?

When I got back to these blessed shores (there's nothing like going abroad to make you appreciate Scotland) I phoned around to try to find out what passports are meant to do. The Foreign Office was cautious, merely pointed out that as a document it was the property of the Government, but conferred no rights in other countries. The Greek Embassy listened politely to my tirades, and said that unless there were reciprocal agreements with other countries waiving the necessity for passports, you had to have one and that was that.

But I remembered, with chauvinistic satisfaction, that when we had Arthur Blessit, the American hippie preacher, on a *Mainly Magnus* programme last winter, he forgot his passport too. The immigration authorities at Prestwick and at London allowed him to enter the country freely, and leave it again, without one.

That's what I call freedom. And democracy.

June, 1972

Magnus and the late Sir Eric Thompson contemplate the problems of filming the temple at Tikal

16

The Quest for a Dump
of Gold

I SUPPOSE if businessmen have a Mecca, a Shangri-La, it's Eldorado;
not the county in California or the various towns in Latin America
and the US, named in wistful hope of some elusive prosperity, but
the Eldorado of legend in Colombia. It grew from a fable of some
chieftain of an Indian town near Bogota who every year would take
part in a ritual purification ceremony, during which he would
plaster his body with resin and then rub himself all over with gold
dust. He would then be taken out on to Lake Guatavita, where he
would plunge into the water to wash off the dust.

His people would also throw gold plate and precious objects into
the waters of the lake in an orgy of purification; and as the chieftain
plunged naked into the lake, they would modestly turn their backs
and throw stones into the water over their shoulders—except that,
being in Colombia, the stones happened to be emeralds.

It was a story to whet the greedy appetites of the Spanish
Conquistadores who invaded Latin America early in the 16th
century. Soon practically every Spaniard in the place was searching
for this fabulous "gilded man," Eldorado himself, especially when
one yarn-spinner claimed to have been entertained by him in a city
called Omagua.

Gradually the stories improved, until "Eldorado" had become a
whole fabulous country of gold with two cities, Omagua and
Manoa. Gonzalo Pizarro hastened over from Peru to join in the
hunt. So did Orellana, who sailed down the Amazon, and de
Quesada. Sir Walter Raleigh himself tried to find Manoa in the
Orinoco lowlands in 1595. Throughout the 17th century, the golden

city of Eldorado was actually shown on maps variously in Brazil and the Guianas.

Others simply tried to test the story by diving into Lake Guatavita itself. In 1571, a Spaniard got a concession from the King of Spain to try to drain the lake by cutting away part of its retaining wall. He didn't succeed in draining it dry, but he paid the king a tax on what he found of some $175,000 in modern equivalent—and since the tax was 20 per cent of the total profit, it means he must have dredged up valuables to the tune of some $875,000.

Certainly, some odd things have happened there. One superb ornament has been found, it's claimed, showing a golden man on a solid gold raft. Lots of people have tried their hand at getting at the secrets of the lake. In 1913, a £90,000 company was formed in London to go out to the lake and dredge it. The seekers bored a tunnel into the side of the lake to drain it, hoping to scoop out all the silt at the bottom. What happened to that expedition is a bit of a mystery, because the members claimed they found nothing, and all the original shareholders lost their shirts. But local villagers are full of stories of a moonlight flit one night; they say the hunters found boxes and boxes of emeralds and golden ornaments, and left very suddenly with all the loot.

Well, that's the sort of story you'd expect to hear. But in 1965 an American diver explored the lake and came up with 25 pieces of gold and ceramics. And this very summer, a new and very high-powered expedition is being mounted by an American treasure-hunter in a once-and-for-all bid to solve the secret of Eldorado. He's a man called Norman Scott, a young, energetic entrepreneur, who is leading a quiet revolution in the traditional and rather conservative world of archaeology. He's introducing for the first time on a very large scale, industrial sponsorship of digs, or rather dives.

One of the results of this kind of sponsorship we showed in the BBC's archaeology programme, *Chronicle*—the exploration of the sacred sacrificial well at the Mayan city of Chichen Itza, in central America. The Maya, who flourished from around the time of the birth of Christ until the arrival of the Spanish invaders in the 16th century, used to throw human sacrifices (usually children) and costly votive offerings to the rain-gods who were supposed to inhabit its murky waters, and Norman Scott, like many treasure-hunters before him, wanted to get his hands on the loot.

But the problem, as always, was how to finance the operation. In the early days of archaeology, excavations were financed by wealthy men themselves, like Heinrich Schliemann, the German grocer's son who eventually excavated Homer's Troy and Mycenae, or like Sir Arthur Evans, who spent a quarter of a million pounds of his own private fortune in excavating and restoring the Minoan palace of Knossos, in Crete. Then museums and universities got in on it, financing specialised expeditions. But they always had a motive—they needed tangible results in the form of treasure or artefacts for their shelves, and it led to some unseemly looting of sites and smuggling of finds out of hostile countries. Some digs are financed by public subscription and local socieites; the best example of this, perhaps, is the series of digs in search of King Arthur's Camelot. Even though you only want to investigate an Iron Age hill-fort (such as South Cadbury Hill), you need only mention the magic words "Arthur" and "Camelot" and the money comes flowing in from impassioned members of Arthurian societies who secretly believe that Arthur still lives and will come back one day to lead Britain into a golden millennium.

Norman Scott tried a different method—and it worked. He got the money from industry; many different industries.

Sir Eric inspects a Maya wall painting

First of all he gets government permission to explore the site, under the supervision of expert native archaeologists—the Chichen Itza dives were supervised by the National Museum of Mexico, for Scott himself is not an archaeologist. Then he sells the story in advance to the various media—the *National Geographic*, the *Observer* colour supplement, and so on. Then he sells the film of the story to the television networks like CBS and the BBC. All this, of course, before a penny has been raised—it's all contingent.

Having done that, he makes approaches to industry. First of all, there's the sophisticated modern equipment required, and it goes without saying that he gets the use of it free from the manufacturers concerned. Purex, the filtering firm, provided all the equipment required for purifying the water in the sacred well at the rate of a million gallons a day. Ford's provided the 21 vehicles required to transport the expedition on the 3,000-mile drive from Florida to the Yucatan peninsula—a spectacular cavalcade that made headlines along the whole journey. And so on.

In addition, the companies actually paid money for the privilege of simply having their names appear in the film and press stories. No hard-sell, just a prestige exposure of their products, like Rolex watches for the divers. Sums like $50,000 went gladly into the kitty,

The filming is over at Chichen Itza: downhill all the way

until Scott had raised a million dollars from industry and the media, and set to work.

That's how he is going to look for Eldorado this summer. The beauty of it is, from the archaeological point of view, that he doesn't absolutely require to find anything. Whatever he finds is automatically the property of the National Museum of the country he is working in. There is no temptation to conceal finds in order to sell them on the black market later to recoup his costs.

It's clearly a much better method than, for instance, the situation in Northern Ireland, where the Belgian diver Robert Stenuit, a trained archaeologist and professional diver as well, has found an Armada wreck, the galleass *Girona,* strewn with gold coins and precious objects. He is financed by a business consortium in Marseilles; but it will be years and years before the courts decide who owns the find. The Board of Trade claims it as shipwreck; Stenuit claims it as personal possessions of drowned passengers. Eventually he will either get a third of the value as salvage—probably about £300,000—or the whole lot, depending on which way the legal argument is settled. And thereafter, some government, in Ireland or Spain, will have to find the money to buy the treasure from him and set up a museum for it.*

But just a minute, you may be saying: what's in it for me, the industrialist? Why should I spend the firm's money sponsoring prestige excavations?

Well, in the first place I would call to mind the dictum of that spectacular newspaperman, Randolph Hearst, who told all his editors: "I want three things in my papers—sex, money, and archaeology." He knew a good selling-line when he saw one, did Hearst. People are fascinated by archaeology; the number of books on archaeology published each year is awe-inspiring—and they sell like hot cakes. The French archeological periodical *Archaeologia* sells more than 60,000 copies each issue—and it is only one of literally dozens of magazines devoted to the subject. The great digs—and there are many of them going on right now—touch some

---

*The *Girona* story had a particularly happy ending. The treasures recovered by Stenuit were bought in 1971 by the Ulster Museum in Belfast for £132,000. Of that sum, £88,000 was supplied by a special grant from the former Northern Ireland government, the rest was raised by public subscriptions and donations. The whole *Girona* collection is now on display in the Ulster Museum.

extraordinarily responsive chord in our imaginations; digging up the past has an adventure and a glamour that is difficult to explain but impossible to ignore.

So the industrialist looking for prestige soft-sell "exposure" has a ready-made interest to invest in. Look at the miles of newsprint that were devoted to the discovery of the beautiful Celtic silverware on St Ninian's Isle in Shetland!

There are plenty of sites in Scotland begging to be excavated, if only the money were there. In the Orkneys, there's a whole empty island called Auskerry that is absolutely thick with suggestive sites, including what may be a Viking ship-burial—which would be the first ship-burial found in Britain since the heady days of the excavation of the Sutton Hoo ship and its spectacular treasures in 1938. Oil companies, are you listening?

January, 1970

17

Gazing at the Navel of the World

FROM THE Navel of the World, as Easter Island has somewhat fancifully been called, I have to report that Thor Heyerdahl of Kon-Tiki fame is a load of rubbish.

Harsh words, you say. Strong words. How could Heyerdahl, that Norwegian darling of the armchair explorers, be a load of rubbish? Had he not, in 1947, made an epic voyage on a soggy, waterlogged balsa-wood raft from Peru westwards across the Pacific to the atoll of Raroia in the Tuamotu Archipelago of French Oceania? Had he not thereby proved that Polynesia had been settled by American Indians from the New World, rather than by seafaring peoples from Asia? And had not his subsequent archaeological expedition to Easter Island itself in 1956 clinched his argument that the original settlers of Polynesia were the Incas from Peru, rather than DPs from the southern coasts of China?

The answer, in a word, is No.

Oh, he made the epic journey all right, back in 1947—he and four companions, drifting for 101 days on a westbound current from South America before capsizing on the jagged reefs that encircle Raroia atoll. Oddly enough, he had the greatest difficulty in finding a British publisher for the book he wrote to celebrate his feat, until in 1950 Allen & Unwin took it on spec and found themselves, to their gratified surprise, with a bestseller on their hands; the postwar public, it turned out, was eager for a dash of swashbuckling adventure, and Heyerdahl was setting a new trend for sponsored journeys that is only now beginning to slacken its hold on our interest.

The Press seized on the story and accepted it uncritically at the face-value that Heyerdahl put on it—namely, that here at last was

Magnus and Professor Colin Renfrew and Easter Island statue

the proof, the incontrovertible proof, of a rather tired old theory
that anthropologists had long since shot down in flames—the South
American origins of Polynesian society.

In actual fact, of course, he had proved no such thing. He had
simply proved that in 1947 it was possible for five men on a balsa-log
raft equipped with hundreds of cans of food, radios, maps, solar
stills to make drinking water from the sea, modern navigational
instruments and so on, to survive for 101 days on a drifting current if
they were tough enough and brave enough to attempt it.

Unfortunately, the Peruvians never used rafts with sails, such as
Heyerdahl used, until *after* the Spanish Conquest. They certainly
used rafts for coastal voyages long before the Spaniards came, but
they were propelled by paddles; and would they have carried water
and supplies for 100 days for normal coastal voyages?—because
without that, they would have died on their accidental way to
Polynesia.

Of course, Heyerdahl adduced considerably more evidence to
support his theory in his Polynesian expeditions. The major factor
on which he relied was the presence in Polynesia of the sweet potato
(the *kumara*) which is of South American origin. This, however,
could just as well have been introduced into Polynesia *after* the
Spanish Conquest from the Old World, as into Peru by Polynesian
voyagers *before* the Conquest. Heyerdahl also made much of an
alleged similarity between the blood-types of the Peruvians and the
Eastern Polynesians. Unfortunately, Polynesians are now so
intermixed that no such thing as a "pure" Polynesian type remains,
and it is well-known that peoples of the most physically diverse and
unrelated races can have similar blood-groups; for instance, the
Eskimos of Labrador have blood-group frequencies practically
identical with the aborigines of Australia! In point of fact,
Peruvians are short, barrel-chested, coppery, straight-haired and
with hooked noses, while Polynesians are tall, brown, stocky, with
wavy black hair and flat wide noses. There is simply no genetic
resemblance between them.

On the other hand, there is considerable evidence to indicate that
there were no pre-Conquest contacts between Polynesia and Peru.
Take the matter of diseases, for instance.

In prehistoric Polynesia, leprosy was endemic; but it was not
found amongst South American Indians until it was introduced by

Europeans there. In the same way, venereal disease was completely unknown in Polynesia until it was introduced by Europeans, whereas it was endemic amongst American Indians. Indeed venereal disease was a strictly American Indian disease, and was unknown in Europe until it was brought back from South America by the early European explorers.

Perhaps what finally misled Heyerdahl into falling hook, line and sinker for his discredited theory was his first sight of the astonishing sculptured statues of Easter Island. They really are breathtaking— huge towering statues of men with long ears, originally set up on massive stone platforms as idols but now all knocked down by rival groups long before Heyerdahl arrived. They look mournful now, lying in pieces about the platforms; but in a quarry in the centre of the island you can see them upright still—and what an astonishing scene they present.

Rano Raraku is an ancient volcanic crater, and this was where the ancient Easter Islanders had their statue factory. They literally carved the statues out of the rock-faces; most of them are about 30 feet high, but one unfinished giant is 70 feet long. Having gouged these monstrous statues from the stone, they were manhandled down the steep face of the crater and raised to allow the back to be completed; after that they were trundled off, on rollers no doubt, hauled by myriads of islanders, to be set up on ceremonial platforms all round the island.

At Rano Raraku, more than 400 of these statues are lying around in all stages of completion, from the very first incisions to the completed statue all ready for transportation. On either side of the road leading away from the quarry, statues lie discarded every fifty yards. It was as if one day this whole massive statue-making industry came to an abrupt halt. The assembly line—and it *was* an assembly line—simply downed tools.

Nowhere else in all Polynesia can one find these awe-inspiring statues. And Thor Heyerdahl leapt to a conclusion: the Easter Islanders must have learned these monumental skills from the Incas. They must have been an Inca people who brought this knowledge with them. Heyerdahl postulated that the original settlers were Tiahuanaco Indians (from Bolivia, actually!), led by the god Kon-Tiki Viracocha.

Unfortunately, the archaeological evidence now proves that the

first settlers of Easter Island arrived around 400 AD—whereas the Tiahuanaco culture did not develop in South America until 750 AD. Similarly, the god Kon-Tiki Viracocha may date back to 750 AD but only rose to prominence as an Inca god around 1500 AD. (The Tiahuanaco culture, by the way, included fine pottery—but no pottery has ever been found on Easter Island). The Tiahuanaco Indians built large buildings and had large statues, but they bear not the slightest resemblance to Easter Island statues. And finally, the monumental masonry of the platforms that at first glance looks so reminiscent of the Inca culture was not developed by the Incas until about 1500 AD.

So, according to Heyerdahl, the first Polynesians were Peruvians who arrived in 400 AD led by an Inca god of 750 AD and with a Tiahuanaco culture of 750 AD (without pottery), building Inca platforms of 1500 AD, speaking Polynesian and not Peruvian, and without venereal disease, using sail-propelled non-Peruvian rafts that were never thereafter adopted by the Polynesians. It's all rather confusing.

As I say, Thor Heyerdahl is a load of rubbish.

But enough of the past. What of the present? The present, alas, is rather sad. And for that one can totally blame the appalling effect of European civilisation. Europe destroyed Easter Island.

It was in 1722 that the first Europeans set eyes on Easter Island: a Dutch exploring expedition who arrived on Easter Sunday and named the island because of that. They spent one day on the island, admired the great stone statues, and shot a few of the natives as a matter of course. Fifty years later, a Spanish expedition arrived, in 1770, and claimed Easter Island for the Spanish crown. Captain Cook paid a lightning visit in 1774, the French came in 1786. Early in the 19th century an American schooner came looking for colonists for a sealing-station on the Robinson Crusoe island off Chile, Juan Fernandez, and managed to capture a score of "volunteers" from Easter Island after a fierce struggle.

Visiting ships thereafter met a hostile reception. But by 1862 the islanders' suspicion of the outside world had lessened, and in that year a flotilla of seven Peruvian ships arrived. Unknown to the islanders, they were slave-hunters; and when they sailed away on Christmas Eve, they had a thousand slaves in their holds, who were sold off to dig guano on the Galapagos islands off Peru. There was such an outcry over this that the authorities decided the slaves should be released and taken back; but by then 900 of them were already dead, and 85 of the surviving hundred died on the voyage back. So only 15 came back to Easter Island. They brought back with them smallpox, which spread like wildfire throughout the island; soon the population of Easter Island had dwindled to a mere 111 men, women, and children. Before the Europeans arrived, there had been 4,000.

It is a sorry and tragic tale. At the end of the last century, the island was annexed by Chile for its sheep-grazing potential, and now Easter Island is very much part of Chile, with a Governor and all—and with Chile's astonishing financial problems as well. The official rate of exchange for the US dollar is 70 escudos—but the unofficial black market rate is 600 escudos. Prices are based on the unofficial rate (my hotel room was 64 dollars a *night*), but have to be paid at the official rate. It would be all right if you could pay in black market rates; but alas for would-be currency speculators, there are armed soldiers at the airport bank to ensure that you have official bank receipts for all your escudos—or else.

The population has risen to about 3,000 now, and twice-weekly air services from Chile and Tahiti are beginning to open up the island to tourists. But it's still a beaten place, its traditional culture snuffed out so cruelly. The fallen statues are mute reminders of a vigorous past, when fine builders and artists created a soaring and ambitious culture. Inter-village rivalry caused the downfall of the statues—perhaps helped by an uprising against the elitist "long-ears" who demanded reverence and worship from the peasantry. But it was Europe and Europeans who did the mortal damage to Easter Island, to our lasting shame; it is now up to the white man to help Easter Island back on its feet.

Archaeology, in a way, is doing just that. Slowly, year by year, the truth about Easter Island's mysterious past is being revealed. And a people with a past have always got a future. That past, despite Thor Heyerdahl, may not be as spectacularly romantic as has been supposed; but it is truly Polynesian, and to me that's a whole lot better than being mythically Peruvian.

July, 1973

The Flying Pegasus which, as Magnus predicted, captured the headlines and attention at the great Chinese Exhibition in London in 1973

18

When the Year of the Ox became
the Year of the Horse

THE Year of the Ox, they say it is. But to my mind it is to be the Year of the Horse: more specifically, a small bronze statuette of a horse galloping at such speed he hardly touches the ground, a spiritual Pegasus.

This beautiful work of art, I predict, is going to take Britain by storm. It is only eighteen inches long. One flailing hoof steps lightly on the back of a flying swallow, the others scythe the air. The impression of grace and swiftness is uncanny. It is a masterpiece. And it is nearly 2,000 years old.

It will be the star performer in a spectacular exhibition of Chinese archaeological treasures at the Royal Academy at Burlington House, in Picadilly, London, a year or so after the Tutankhamun Exhibition at the British Museum. This Chinese Exhibition, which comes to London after a preliminary canter in Paris, is going to out-Tut even Tut.

It won't, of course, have the peculiar emotional advantages that gave the Tut Exhibition its special appeal—the mystery and vulnerability of a boy-king of whom almost nothing was known except that his face was unforgettable, and the dramatic circumstances of the finding and excavation of his almost unplundered tomb long after Egyptologists had given up hope of ever finding an intact Royal Egyptian burial.

But it will have a lot of other things going for it.

Size, for one thing. The Tut exhibition had 50 exhibits; the Chinese one will have anything up to 500.

And for another, a burial tomb (two tombs, in fact) of a Prince and Princess of the Western Han dynasty whose funerary treasures put Tut's tomb in the shade.

They were discovered in 1968, at Man-ch'eng in Hopei Province. But news of the discovery took a long time to filter to the western world, for China was then in the throes of the Great Cultural Revolution and was totally enclosed. Western archaeologists had no way of knowing what was happening behind China's borders, and feared the worst.

But it turned out that the revolutionaries were digging away with tremendous zeal. The excavation report reads like nothing else imaginable, for all virtue and credit is given where it ideologically belongs. As follows:

> This archaeological work was done with the deep concern of the Central Committee of the Communist Party headed by Chairman Mao. The officers and men of the Chinese People's Liberation Army were the first to discover one of the tombs. They immediately reported their find to the authorities, meanwhile carefully guarding the site. With the close co-operation between the Institute of Archaeology of the Chinese Academy of Sciences and the Archaeological Team of Hopei Province and thanks to vigorous support and assistance from the PLA and the local revolutionary masses, this tomb was excavated.

(No nonsense here about letting effete aristocrats like Lord Caernarvon or unenlightened grubbers like Howard Carter get any credit).

The occupant of the first tomb was Liu Sheng, Prince Ching of Chungshan, dating from the 2nd century BC. The tomb was literally an underground palace hewn deep into rocky cliffs; it was more than 150 feet long and 25 feet high, comprising four massive chambers at the end of a long passage. The antechamber held several chariots and a dozen horses still at the shafts, which had been slaughtered after being driven inside. There were several hundred pieces of earthenware for holding food and wine to keep the Prince in provisions in the afterlife.

The two tombs, of Liu Sheng and his wife Tou Wan, who had been buried in a similar underground palace nearby, contained nearly 3,000 funeral objects, including bronze vessels, gold, silver, iron and jade articles, lacquerware and silks.

But as with Tutankhamun, it was the coffins of the princely pair that created the most spectacular impact. Each of the corpses had

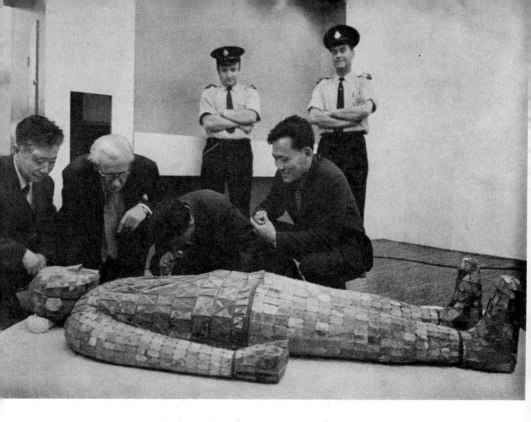

The death-suit of Princess Tou Wan

been sewn into a suit made up of 2,500 plates of jade sewn together with gold thread.

But Liu Sheng and his wife got none of the sympathy from the archaeologists that Tutankhamun has always aroused. He was the elder brother of the Emperor Wu Ti of Han, and was notorious for his depravity and corruption, his lust for women and wine, and he levied exorbitant taxes on the 600,000 people in his fiefdom. The Chineses archaeologists were uncompromising in their interpretation of the finds: "This discovery was a penetrating exposure of the idle and extravagant life of the feudal ruling class based on their cruel oppression and exploitation of the labouring people . . . and at the same time show the skill and hard work of the labouring people in such early times." They never miss a trick. I can just imagine how very differently Howard Carter would have written up his discovery of Tut's tomb had he been thus ideologically orientated.

Whether visitors to the Exhibition see the treasures as examples of "cruel exploitation" or "the wisdom of China's labouring people of ancient times," they are going to have their breath taken away. In the last five years, an enormous number of archaeological sites have been discovered and excavated in China, each one more spectacular than the last. The Flying Pegasus, found in a tomb in the Province of Kan-su and dating from the 1st century AD, is only one of literally thousands of such priceless finds.

Paintings, vases, statuettes, early manuscripts of Confucius, ceramics, porcelains, silks—the scale and range of China's archaeological revolution has been fantastic. Yet it's a very new subject in China, compared with the west. It was not until 1920 that the first archaeological excavations were undertaken in China, by a Swedish mining engineer called Gunnar Andersson, who uncovered a Stone Age site in the Yellow River area. This opened the floodgates. Archaeologists ranged backwards and forwards in time. They discovered the earliest known man of the time—Peking Man, 500,000 years old—and excavated the older parts of Peking itself that Marco Polo had visited when it was called Tatu in the late 13th century (he called it the largest city he had ever seen, and praised its perfect town planning and chessboard layout).

Whatever other countries can boast in the way of archaeological specialities, the Chinese, apparently, can cap it now. China has even had its Abu Simbel (the rock temples on the Nile that were bodily dismantled and reassembled on higher ground when threatened by submersion under the waters of the Aswan Dam).

A huge new dam was planned for the San Men Gorge, in the area of the middle reaches of the Yellow River. A vast area known to be archaeologically rich would be submerged, so the Chinese planned and executed an archaeological drive of exemplary breadth and scope.

First, folklorists were sent in to examine and record on the spot all local folk-tales and legends and oral memories of treasures and tombs that might have come to light through ploughing down the centuries. Huge teams of local peasants, using poles tipped with a hollow metal ferrule, made borings in every single square yard of the area, each bore bringing up a core of earth that showed whether there was a "floor" of occupation underneath the surface. By this means, archaeologists were able to plot the subterranean strata of the whole region.

Then the excavations began. At Shan-ts'un-ling the royal cemetery of the state of Kuo before 655 BC was uncovered—234 tombs, no less, crammed with treasures—and all were cleared and carried to safety before the waters came. And all this without massive UNESCO finance, as in the case of Abu Simbel, of course.

There is still an immense amount of archaeological work to be done in China, quite clearly. But already enough has been done to clarify vast misty areas of inscrutable history that had formerly been half dismissed as legend and myth. Chinese scholarship until the last fifty years was a hidebound literary tradition that hinted at marvels of civilisation that no one else could accept as possibly being true. Now archaeology is putting these historical legends into perspective—and showing that they had a lot of truth in them after all, just as Heinrich Schliemann did for the Homeric civilisation of Troy and Mycenae, and as Sir Arthur Evans did for Minoan Crete.

The fact that the Chinese Government is now beginning to release detailed information about the archaeological revolution of the past few years is immensely encouraging—as, indeed, is the mere fact of the prospect of the great Exhibition in London later this year. China is opening up at last to the west, just as her history is opening up to the digger's spade.

March, 1973

19

To the Great Wall of China
—and back

As WE HUMPED our baggage off the train at Hong Kong, my companion said, "Keep an eye on your bags—you're not in Communist China now, you know."

And it seemed to me to summarise entirely the difference between two worlds. Communism and capitalism. Turning the quick dollar, and overturning the world of the quick dollar.

We had just spent three weeks together filming in China—the New China, as they keep insisting—for a BBC film series that will go out this autumn in association with the great Exhibition of Chinese Treasures I have already extolled in these pages. It was my first visit not just to China, but to the Far East. And I was staggered. Bowled over.

China simply isn't Oriental at all. All these fantasies I had about the Far East—you know, bazaars and beggars, pickpockets and cut-throats, endless haggling and extortionate tipping—where were they? I saw no drunks, no beggars. There was no tipping (ah, blessed relief!). No theft, in that I never had to lock an hotel door. No dogs.

No real dirt, in the sense that India is filthy. Just tidiness, order, neatness, cleanliness—and method. After three weeks of it, Hong Kong came as a gaudy, garish and (but whisper it) welcome shock. What one misses in the New China is the reek of Western decadence.

I have just traversed China from Peking and its Forbidden City in the north-west, up to the Great Wall built at such fearful sacrifice of human life in the fourth century BC (or was it the third?), down into the "Yellow Earth" heartlands of Central China where the first civilisations began to bloom 4,000 years ago, and then right down to the south, to the steamy tropical jungles of Canton as the jumping-off point for Hong Kong.

It was a tremendous experience. Not exciting, in the sense that some countries are exciting. But eye-opening, impressive, unforgettable. My mind is a bewildering jumble of kaleidoscopic impressions. China is such an extraordinary mixture of the old and the new.

So first of all, let's get the vocabulary right. In China you talk about "after Liberation," which means after the Communist victory over Chiang Kai Chek in 1949. Everything in China is either pre-Liberation or post-Liberation. Philosophical readers may want to query the word "Liberation," for though it freed the rent-racked peasants (who represent 85 per cent of China's 800 millions), it also shackled all free thought, all artistic expression, all criticism. This column is not a place for political debate, however. Yet . . . yet . . . how sad it is that the nation that invented writing, paper, printing and books does not now print any books for public consumption except the thoughts of Chairman Mao, banal as they are, and exhortatory comics. How sad it is that the nation that invented porcelain and some of the finest art forms the world has ever seen should have proscribed the aesthetic and the beautiful.

My journey through China, in which I was studying Chinese antiquity, was shot through with bronze and jade and silk and gold, the beautiful objects that will be on display in London this autumn. Yet it all comes to an abrupt stop at Liberation.

So did many other things. Sex, for instance. I hesitate to be so blunt in these columns, but Axiom No. 1 for all businessmen visiting China is that *there is no sex in China.* The new China is intensely puritanical. There is no word in the classical Chinese language for "kissing" (I dare not go further), and 20th century translations of modern novels had to invent a word for "pushing mouths together." Women here wear baggy, shapeless trousers and tunics that deny their femininity. Men wear the same. Everywhere, the blue uniform of Maoism. No one holds hands in public. No one kisses in public. And the prescribed family is two children, no more. Otherwise you are in for a bit of "self-criticism" in front of the Commune. That's Women's Lib for you.

This imposed puritanism is symptomatic of many revolutions from Cromwell onwards. But what happens to that powerful procreative instinct with which we are born? Is it sublimated into mortification, as in the days of the early Christians and latter-day

Catholic priesthood ? Is it something that revolutionary régimes fear in case it takes the edge off idealistic fervour, in the way that athletes aren't meant to have sex for days and days before a contest? I don't know. Perhaps, in the long run, what matters now to a young Chinese chap is the precise way in which a young Chinese girl adjusts the Red Star on her cap. A kind of neo-Victorianism? Not an ankle, but a cap?

The analogy may not be so far-fetched, for certain aspects of the new China are enchantingly Victorian. The hotels, for instance. Even post-Liberation, they have been built with soaring ceilings and elaborately incompetent plumbing, great useless pieces of furniture, just like the railway hotels in their heyday. And the railways themselves. Despite the classless society, there are two classes of travel—Hard, and Soft. We travelled Soft, and it was a delight. Pullman-type coaches of the old style, with banquettes for sleeping in. Long, leisurely, comfortable journeys, pulled by steam-driven dinosaurs that blew their bewitching cries far into the night, echoing over the stupendous vistas of this land.

This land. China is *about* land. A quarter of the world's population in a country the size of Canada. Everywhere the land is sculpted into elaborate terraces, to conserve precious water and create cultivable terrain where none existed before. It's been going on since the Stone Age—and it's going on still.

But it's a dusty place, this land. The dust of centuries blows over it, lies upon it, almost smothers it at times. The people go about in gauze masks, to intercept not only dust but also bacteria and germs and viruses, for the Chinese are intensely hypochondriac and have the benefit of some of the most advanced medical treatment in the world. But it all adds to the austere, grey impression that cities like Peking give you. The Forbidden City within it, the old palace precincts of the Dragon Emperors, is now a public museum—*that's* what gives Peking its only touch of colour and elegance. Everything else is grey and functional, the old houses low and cowering (for no house was allowed to be higher than the imperial palace), the new ones simple boxes built to house the workers. Worse than Drumchapel.

Peking doesn't feel like a city at all. For one thing, there is the weird absence of motor cars. There are no privately-owned cars in China: only official vehicles. So they are few and far between.

Instead, you have myriads of bicycles—1,700,000 in Peking alone, I was told, in a population of 7 million—which have to be licensed and have to park in special parking lots at ½p a time. Even so, the air is raucous with motor horns, because the cyclists treat the roads like jay-walkers, and Peking drivers drive with their thumbs firmly pressed on the hooter.

And instead of hoardings exhorting us to buy this or see that, there are massive posters advertising a Thought from the Chairman: Peoples of the world unite, Work for the Revolution, and so on. I'm not sure that there is any real difference between the two kinds of hoardings—both are designed to manipulate the mind, the one for the good of private enterprise, the other for the good, arguably, of the State, or at least the Communist Party.

I don't suppose I can claim to have seen the *real* China (question: what is the real China?). We travelled, as it were, in a gilded, insulated cage, with interpreters and Foreign Office "guides" always hovering at our elbows. We did not see many of the places we asked to see. We were not tourists, for such a thing as tourism doesn't exist in China yet. We were treated as honoured guests, with elaborate courtesies to undergo at every stop while stupefying reams of statistics were read over us. We were shown only what the Chinese wanted us to see—the best. (I can't say I blame them: my own blood boils when a London film crew comes to Glasgow, say, or the Highlands, and shows only the shortcomings and none of the advantages).

But once we were out in the country, what we saw was undeniably impressive. We were shown a People's Commune some 25 kilometres from Sian, in Central China, where 14 villages, some 14,000 people in all, had been yoked into 14 teams of "productive brigades." They were busy building a series of linked reservoirs that would enable the villagers to have two crops a year instead of only one—rice as well as millet. "Before Liberation, the peasants could eat only half the year, the rest of the time they lived off wild vegetables," said the interpreter. Since Liberation, they have doubled production.

I watched them at work. They were building a huge earth reservoir practically with their bare hands. Loudspeakers blared martial music and exhortations. Teams vied with each other. It was back-breaking work, hauling the soil up the ramparts. This was not collectivisation, it was insectivisation. But it was working. They all looked happy—honestly. The headiness of revolution and liberation has not worn off. And I found myself mourning the loss of national drive in the west, the lack of patriotic pride—mourning the days of certainty and pride in prowess.

For there is in China, to my mind, a kind of innocence still, the innocence we have lost. I'm not talking here of party politics and infighting, of which I know nothing. There is the innocence of pioneers, and Methodists, and Quakers. The innocence of fable. All history is reduced to fable, and reinforced by fable. Such, one feels, were the Children of Israel as they wandered the Middle East in days of old: obsessed, unshakeably convinced in the rightness of their fable. And their formula.

It is very hard, when in China, to think of China as an expansionist or aggressive power. There is so much for them to do right there in their homeland. The Chinese themselves come across as rather jolly and rather earnest at the same time; rather affectionate and rather reserved at the same time. A strange and ambiguous mixture. It is impossible not to like them, not to like

Spectacular new finds from China: a terracotta army of lifesize warriors buried to protect the tumulus of China's first Emperor, discovered in 1974

their laughter and their essentially banana-skin sense of fun, not to like and secretly envy the essential simplicity of their vision.

It's not exhilarating. It's even a little dreary. But then you cross the frontier to Hong Kong, and the ugly, corrupt, hysterical realities of Westernised Eastern life hit you smack between the eyes. You know you ought to disapprove, to deplore the veniality of it all. But you see the Union Jack fluttering at the railway station, you sip your first (exorbitantly expensive) gin and tonic for three weeks, and you sigh, "It's great to be back in civilisation!"

Then the whining porters try to rob you blind—and you wonder.

May, 1973

20

Whatever happened to Atlantis?

IT'S AMAZING what a wee handful of soil can do. It can overturn history, undermine a pyramid of hypotheses, refute an age of arguments, and generally make everyone look a little silly.

I have just been paying yet another visit to my two favourite Greek islands, Crete and Santorini. It's almost become an annual event. For Santorini (the ancients called it Thera) is turning into the great running story of archaeology, and I keep having to go back and see what else is turning up and dutifully report it all in *Chronicle* on the telly.

For the past five years, Greek archaeologists have been excavating there a new Pompeii—a major city called Akrotiri that was buried under a tremendous mantle of volcanic ash around the year 1500 BC, when the volcano on Santorini exploded in the biggest eruption on earth since the last Ice Age.

Right across the roots of the volcano lay a fine Minoan Bronze Age city: a place of great luxury and wealth, handsome mansions and paved streets, shops and courtyards and workshops, all supplied with the latest in plumbing mod cons: a Knossos for commoners, in effect. It is the earliest known city in Europe, and has aroused tremendous excitement in archaeological circles.

And as for the frescoes! Whereas the Minoan frescoes in Knossos were all smashed to rubble and had to be put together in thousands of fragments and quite a lot of guesswork and reconstruction, the frescoes of Santorini are practically unscathed, glowing with colour and grace and life, each a greater masterpiece than the last.

But what gives Santorini its special compulsive attraction is the theory that has been growing fashionable even in academic circles lately, that Santorini, or at least the Santorini eruption, gave birth to the original haunting legend of Atlantis.

Remember Atlantis? Plato wrote up the story in the 4th century BC, based on a story he claimed had been handed down to him from

Santorini: the cliff-top town of Phira, and some of the artefacts found in the buried Minoan city of Akrotiri

his ancestor Solon, who had got it from some priests in Egypt two hundred years earlier. Or so Plato said.

The priests had allegedly told Solon that once upon a time, when the world was very young, there had been a great island empire far to the west. It was larger than Libya and Asia put together, and so powerful that it ruled parts of the continent as well. It was peopled by an immaculate society, the noblest and fairest race of men that ever lived. They were blessed by the gods, particularly their patron god, Poseidon the earth-shaker, and grew prosperous and wealthy in wisdom and justice. They granted due respect to the god, and as part of their reverence for him, their kings would grapple unarmed with bulls, the beasts of Poseidon.

But then they fell from grace, grew greedy and domineering, became arrogant and lustful for power. And they launched a great invasion of the Mediterranean. Only the Athenians stood up to them (Solon was told), and eventually by sheer heroic valour they defeated the Atlanteans and occupied their island. But the Atlanteans were to be punished even more drastically. For Poseidon, angered by their sins, caused a season of violent earthquakes and floods; and in one terrible day and night the island of Atlantis disappeared into the depths of the sea.

But where had Atlantis been? Plato placed it in time some 10,000 years before his day, which was ridiculous (for Athens hadn't been going for a thousand years by then, far less than ten thousand), and out in the Atlantic, which wasn't.

The search for Atlantis has inspired a whole industry. Books about it have appeared by the score, by the hundred. Atlantis has been confidently identified on the floor of the Atlantic, in central America, in Morocco, in Nigeria, on a submarine reef near Heligoland, in the West Indies, in the Azores, in Ceylon.

But gradually opinion began to harden in favour of a site within the Mediterranean (assuming that Plato wasn't just making it all up as a philosophical exercise in his own lifelong interest in the Utopian state—which is just as likely). With some judicious juggling of Plato's figures and measurements, Atlantis could be squeezed into a Bronze Age bracket in the Aegean, by reducing all Plato's measurements by a factor of ten (poor old Solon simply couldn't count in Egyptian numerals). That made the main plain of Atlantis, where the capital was situated, about the same size as the main plain of Crete, and brought the time scale to a thousand years before Plato—which was about right for the Minoan civilisation.

Interest in this solution quickened spectacularly when the excavation on Santorini started, and evidence began to emerge that Santorini, too, had been a centre of advanced Minoan culture. Especially since Professor Spyridon Marinatos, the veteran Greek archaeologist in charge, had postulated that Minoan Crete had been destroyed by the same natural catastrophe that destroyed Santorini.

Aha! cried the theorists. Problem solved. The Egyptians weren't thinking of Santorini as Atlantis. They were thinking of Minoan Crete. To the Egyptians, the "Keftiu" of Crete were a rather mysterious people, far to the west, immensely wealthy and cultured, a powerful naval empire who ruled the Aegean trade-routes with their ships and grew prosperous accordingly. Suddenly the Minoans seemed to vanish. No Minoan ships came to Egypt any longer. No ships at all, in fact. There had been a holocaust out there, when the sun had been extinguished and the skies were dark with poisonous clouds. And what about all these plagues we've been having in Egypt, then? And the flood wave that opened the Red Sea and let those pesky Israelites escape? (Never mind the dates, I know they don't fit, don't be so pedantic).

Then the news came filtering in. It was awesome. The island of the Minoans had simply been swallowed up in the sea—and there was some truth in that, for the volcano on Santorini simply tore the heart out of the place and left just a gaping hole in the sea. So that's what happened to the Keftiu, was it? What an end. It must have been divine retribution. Come to think of it, they were beginning to get a bit big for their boots, right enough.

Two books on Atlantis have advanced this hypothesis with greater (*Atlantis: The truth behind the legend,* by A. G.

Galanopoulos and Edward Bacon) or lesser (*The End of Atlantis*, by J. V. Luce) dogmatic conviction. And for a lot of people, that just about wrapped the legend up nicely. Q.E.D.

But then the Santorini excavation, which everyone thought had solved the whole thing, turned difficult. Not because of what was being discovered there, but because of something that was *not* being discovered there. And that something was a particular type of pottery known as Late Minoan Ib. Plenty of Late Minoan Ia, but no Late Minoan Ib.

Now you may think of this as being of no account. What's a scragend of LMIb between friends? But to the archaeologist it meant an awful truth: the whole equation had gone horribly wrong.

You see, Late Minoan Ia was current in Crete and Santorini until about 1500 BC. Late Minoan Ib then took over, as fashions do, and lasted until about 1450 BC. Now, there are masses of Late Minoan Ib in every palace centre in Crete, but nary a shard in Santorini. Ergo, Santorini was destroyed in 1500 BC, and Crete in 1450 BC. Ergo, the theory that the Egyptians blended the simultaneous destruction of Santorini and Crete into an amalgamated Atlantis goes up the spout.

Admittedly, the city of Akrotiri on Santorini had been destroyed by earthquake before the volcano erupted, but only a matter of weeks before, it seemed. Certainly not fifty years earlier, there was no evidence for that. Well, said the archaeologists, couldn't there have been two volcanic eruptions? A wee one to put Santorini out of action, and then the monster one that blew a hole in the island and wrecked Crete? Not a chance, said the vulcanologists, not a chance: Santorini is the nicest single-phase, blow-my-top, one-off eruption we've ever had the pleasure of studying.

So the doubts began to rush in again. Maybe Crete hadn't been destroyed by the Santorini eruption at all? Maybe it had been an invading army of Myceneans from mainland Greece, who pulled down all the palaces and set fire to them just for the hell of it? Where was there any evidence of destruction by tidal waves? Or earthquakes? And show me just one particle of volcanic ash that's ever been found on Cretan soil, go on, show me. Whoever thought up that silly rubbish about Atlantis in the Aegean, anyway? Plato was obviously pulling everyone's leg. As Aristotle put it tersely, "The man who dreamed it up made it vanish."

So the whole beautiful edifice of argument and deduction and inference collapsed like a pack of cards, all because of the lack of a piece of pottery.

But all was not, is not, lost, Atlantis-lovers. For here's where the handful of soil comes in. For an amateur British archaeologist called James Money slipped off to Santorini this summer to do a spot of hard thinking and gentle trowelling. There must be a solution, he reckoned. There simply must be, somewhere, the missing clue that would make the archaeological and the vulcanological evidence match up.

So he looked, and looked very hard, and he found what he was looking for. Tucked away in between the topmost ruins of the city and the lowest layers of volcanic ash, he found pockets of soil: real, honest-to-goodness humus. And how could the soil have got there, if there hadn't been a long time between the earthquake destruction and the volcanic eruption—say fifty years, at a guess? In a stroke, he had righted the argument again: Santorini had been wrecked and evacuated after an earthquake about 1500 BC. No one paid much attention to that. And then fifty years later, as the soil gathered over the ruins, the volcano itself blew up—and no one could avoid taking notice of that.

So we're back more or less where we started. Honour saved on all academic sides. But can you imagine how they're all going to start sweating again if Marinatos finds a bit of Late Minoan Ib on Santorini after all? Cat among the pigeons once again.

November, 1972

Professor Marinatos died in 1974 after a fall while he was busy digging at the Akrotiri site, and his grave is now in one of the houses he excavated. Meanwhile, the Atlantis story goes on. A massive international symposium on Santorini and Crete, called "Thera and the Aegean World," was held on board a cruise-ship in 1978, where experts from many different disciplines met to try to resolve the many problems still outstanding. The general consensus seems now to be that Minoan Crete was destroyed not by the after-effects of the Santorini eruption but by a Mycenean invasion, after all. But the Atlantis story could still have been inspired by the double catastrophe that overtook Thera and then Crete. Legend has a way of telescoping events; the story continues. . . .

21

A Million Dollars' Worth of Pot

POT. Not the stuff you smoke, but heady stuff nonetheless, and a good deal more expensive. No, I'm talking about Met-pot—or to be more explicit, the magnificent Greek pot that the Metropolitan Museum of New York bought for just over a million dollars in 1972.

A million dollars. Now, that's a fair amount of scratch. It's not the amount you sign a cheque for every second day of the week. And if the happy day comes when you *do* shell out that sort of money, you want to have a pretty good idea what it is you're buying. Wouldn't you think?

And yet, for the sum of $1,024,000, the New York Met appears to have bought a right pot in a poke.

It was when I was in Rome that I got the story—the inside story, that's to say, because there have been rumblings of it in the newspapers already, particularly in the *New York Times*. But at the Villa Giulia, the major museum of Etruscan finds in Rome, I was told the whole tale by Dr Giovanni Scichilone, the archaeological Director in the Superintendency of the Antiquities of Southern Etruria.

OK, so this is the yarn. In November, 1972, Mr Thomas P. Hoving, director of the Metropolitan Museum of Art in New York, proudly announced the acquisition of one of the most important Greek vases to come on the market for over a hundred years. It was a cylix krater used for mixing wine and water at banquets. It was made in the 6th century BC by a Greek potter called Euxitheos and painted by an artist called Euphronios. A most beautiful thing: the decoration shows a seldom-represented scene from Greek mythology, in which the dead warrior Sarpedon, son of Zeus and a

casualty of the Trojan War, is removed from the battlefield by Sleep and Death, watched by the god Hermes. The other side of the vase shows a group of warriors arming.

Euphronios has been described as the Michelangelo of ancient Greek pottery painters. He signed all his work, and until this one came on the market, only 24 of his works were known. Exultantly, the Met declared that as a result of this great find, the history of art would have to be re-written. The claim was more spectacular than accurate, but it served its purpose—visitors came pouring into the Met to see the pot, and this is the major justification for important new acquisitions by museums, especially in America.

But where had the vase come from? Ah—that's where the rub began.

Dr Dietrich von Bothmer, who is curator of Greek and Roman art at the Met, told somewhat coyly a story that would have strained the credence of a moron. In the spring of 1972, apparently, he had been approached by a "reputable dealer" called Robert Emanuel Hecht, a 53-year-old American who has lived in Rome for the past 25 years (his father founded the celebrated Hecht department-store chain in Baltimore and Washington).

Hecht said he had a vase of incomparable importance in a safe-deposit in Switzerland. Would von Bothmer like to come and see it? Von Bothmer certainly would, and did. He saw it in a garden in Zurich, and was "speechless, bowled over." And decided to buy it.

Now, there are certain laws about the export of antiquities. Turkey, Greece, Egypt, Italy—these are only a few of the countries where objects of antiquity are very strictly controlled. It is illegal to remove them from the country. So it is incumbent on a reputable purchaser, like a museum, to try to find out whether the object for sale has a legal provenance.

Hecht had the answer ready. He had bought it the previous year, he said, from an Armenian dealer in Beirut called Dikran A. Sarrafian, who had inherited the vase, in fragments, from his father, who had exchanged it for a coin collection in London in 1920 (*before* the passing of laws banning the export of antiquities, notice). Three years earlier, apparently, this Mr Sarrafian had decided to emigrate to Australia, so he glued the broken fragments together and sold them to Hecht for a song. (Needless to say, he still hasn't emigrated to Australia).

That was all right by the Met. No laws had been broken. Here was an indubitable Euphronios vase, legally on the market. And although the previous record price for a Greek vase was $160,000, the Met signed a cheque for over a million on September 13, 1972. And everything in the garden seemed to be lovely.

But almost at once, a storm started brewing—in Italy.

It is a curious fact that one of the major sources for early Greek vases is not Greece but Italy; specifically, Etruria. Because the Etruscans, those rather mysterious pre-Roman people, adored Greek pots and imported them in vast numbers—and filled their tombs with them, too.

The main Etruscan cemetery area is in the district of Cerveteri, some 35 miles north of Rome. Here, in an area of 15 square miles, the ground is honeycombed with tombs, few of which have been officially excavated. But a very large number have been unofficially excavated, by local peasants who double as tomb-robbers at night—*tombaroli*. These *tombaroli* keep the black-market in antiquities in Rome and Milan plentifully supplied.

Earlier this year, rumours began to spread in Cerveteri that the Euphronios vase bought by the Met hadn't been found in Greece and sold in London in 1920 at all. It was, said rumour, the fruit of a major illegal excavation of an Etruscan tomb in December, 1971.

A gentleman called Omero Bordo, who was not a tomb-robber of course but knew a thing or two about it, went on Italian television on February 21 of this year to say that he had "heard" that the vase had come from a tomb at Sant-Angelo at Monte Abatone.

Less than a week later, to everyone's intense surprise, came an actual confession. A man called Armando Cenere admitted that he had taken part in robbing the tomb. He said that there were six of them in all, and that they had worked for eight nights, because the tomb was very deep. They had removed many pieces of pottery, and a statue of a winged sphinx. He distinctly remembered, he said, a large fragment of a vase which showed part of a figure of a man bleeding profusely—just like Sarpedon on the Met pot.

Aha! So! The vase had been illegally excavated, then smuggled out of Italy, had it? No, it hadn't, said the Met. The "confession" was obviously trumped up for some devious Italian reason. But rumour in Italy suggested that the tomb-robbers had turned State evidence because they were hopping mad about the fact that Hecht had only given them $8,500 dollars each for the haul—and netted a cool million for himself.

It was now that the Italian authorities, specifically Dr Giovanni Scichilone, came into the picture. They felt understandably insulted by the Met's attitude. They know perfectly well that there is a vast amount of theft and smuggling of Italian antiquities going on. Over the past 30 years, it has been estimated, more than 50,000 works of art, valued at over $400 million, have left the country illegally. In 1972 alone some 6,000 art objects were stolen, mostly from unguarded churches; and the police have said they think that every year Etruscan artefacts valued at more than half a million dollars are being stolen from tombs.

This is not Italy's fault, for no country could guard such an overwhelming treasury of ancient art such as Italy's. It is the fault of museums all over the world, greedy for acquisitions. It is the fault of rich collectors and tourists who want to own beautiful originals—and even the thriving and prosperous faking business in Italy can't cope with the demand.

But Dr Scichilone, as I said, felt insulted. The Hecht story that the Met claimed to have believed really was an insult to the intelligence. So Dr Scichilone declared war on the Met.

It's difficult to see what he could do. In March of this year, the Italian police got an anonymous phone call to say that if they went to a small church near Cerveteri they would find something to their advantage. There, wrapped in a newspaper, they found four fragments of what was clearly a Euphronios vase, and a note to say they came from the Met pot and were leftovers from the illegal

The Villa Giulia houses the finest of Italy's Etruscan treasures

excavation at Sant-Angelo. Fair enough—but what would that prove? There was no provenance for these fragments, any more than for the Met pot itself. The Met could argue that this, too, was a frame-up, even if the fragments fit the Met pot.

Provenance is all. The argument against illegal excavation is that a pot like the Euphronios vase in the Met has something more than merely aesthetic value. If it is properly and systematically excavated, it can tell us something about history. It can tell us something about the culture of the time if it is recorded in its context. What other objects were found in the tomb? Can that help the problems of dating? Can that tell us about the trade, the economy, the taste, of the Etruscans? Can it tell us something about the way they lived, as well as about the way they died?

Dr Scichilone doesn't want to get the pot back from the Met for its own sake. After all, he's got 15,000 Greek pots from Etruscan graves in the Villa Giulia already. No, all he wants is to get the pot back for one day. He will then mark it clearly—Property of the Italian Government, on permanent loan to the Metropolitan Museum. And send it back to the Met.

Thus honour would be satisfied.

Well, I hope he manages it. Because the scale of smuggling and international illegality in antiquities today is alarming. There are millionaire dealers in Switzerland whose vaults are stuffed with treasures, just waiting for a gullible or dishonest buyer.

Museums are perhaps the greatest culprits. John D. Cooley, the curator of ancient art at Cleveland Museum in America, recently and bravely said that 95 per cent of ancient art material in American museums had been smuggled in, one way or another. The British Museum isn't innocent, either. But in America, one new museum opens, on average, every day of the year. And they require collections. Acquisitions.

There is obviously a way in which other museums, whose cellars are stuffed with undisplayed material, could help to stock new museums, and cut out the middlemen dealers who make fortunes from their activities. But it will take time, and new legislation— above all, a belated return to integrity by the museum men who profess to care so much for the art heritage our ancestors have left us.

August, 1973

22

Greenland: the Island of 'Perhaps'

GREENLAND. What a fascinating place! Let me tell you just a little about it, for it is off the beaten track for most people; and yet what fun it is to visit—even if, like the legendary salesman, you are there to try to sell refrigerators to Eskimoes. (Memo to Sales Directors: you would do pretty well—the Eskimoes are very with it indeed).

First, the place. It is held to be the largest island in the world, if you don't call Australia an island—four times the size of France, most of it lying inside the Arctic Circle. Its population, however, is a mere 30,000 or so, plus some 3,000 Danish residents, for Greenland is at present (since 1953) part and parcel of the realm of Denmark.

We flew there from Iceland, landing somewhat precariously at the former American airbase at Narssarssuag (they abandoned it after the war because of weather uncertainties, and now I know why). Narssarssuag is a frontier town: the few buildings, which include a very pleasant hotel, are prefabricated from plain unvarnished concrete, and the transport services are somewhat pragmatic. Just as in some southern countries the operating word is *"mañana"*—"tomorrow"—in Greenland the operating word is *"mahari"*—"perhaps." Tomorrow is when the plane may come back. Tomorrow is when the boat may be available. Perhaps.

"Mahari"—it's the most soothing sound in the world. And a rare corrective for executive ulcers, which think that plane schedules and getting somewhere fast are ends in themselves. In Greenland they are merely the means, and you learn to take them as they come.

Basically, Greenland is a huge lump of ice surrounded by a barely inhabitable coastal fringe. Flying over it, you cannot conceive of any human life there at all. It's a great granite plateau of up to 12,000 feet, spiked with peaks and smothered in an eternal glacier measuring up to two miles in thickness in places. It is here that

American scientists are extracting ice-bores that tell the story of the successive freezes and thaws of the world's climate as vividly as tree-rings.

Yet life there is. Down in the south, where deep fjords have been hacked out of the coastline, there are pleasant grassy valleys where sheep abound and can graze outside for most of the year. There are polar bear to the north and east, reindeer and musk-ox and lemming; but to the south you find almost-tame Arctic hares and foxes, and you might now be surprised to witness a charge of playful yak—yak were introduced to Greenland some ten years ago to see how they would fare, and they're now doing very nicely indeed, thank you. And all around, the surrounding seas teem with seal and walrus and Greenland whale (the largest whale in the world), which the brave Eskimoes used to hunt in their absurdly fragile but beautifully manoeuvrable kayaks.

Today there's less of the hunting than before. Finding a man who can still handle a kayak properly (somersaulting it and all that) is increasingly difficult. The seal alone used to provide for practically all the Eskimo's needs—food, light, heat, clothing, tents, boats. Nowadays the main occupation is fishing, with farming and mining a rapidly-growing alternative (there is uranium there, and cryolite, and some coal farther north).

In fact, nowadays it hardly does to talk about Eskimoes at all. You talk of Greenlanders. They are much the most "advanced" of the Eskimo peoples, even though closely related to the Eskimoes of Canada. They have their own newspaper, their own radio station, their own books and novels, their own schools and college, all under the paternal and paternalistic eye of Denmark, which laid claim to Greenland in 1605.

But before then, as you may know, there had been *another* Greenland—and it was to find this other Greenland that I myself went there. Because for 500 years or so, there was a Nordic settlement in Greenland, sponsored by Iceland and eventually taken over by Norway. And this settlement was one of the most extraordinary human adventures of all time.

It was started by a man called Eirik the Red in the year 985. He was an Icelander who had been exiled for manslaughter, and used his period of banishment to explore and survey this vast and relatively unknown country to the west. It was unoccupied at that time; a warmer climate had driven the ice northward, and with the ice went the seal-hunting Dorset Eskimo. Eirik thought the country inhabitable, and gave it its misleading name of "Greenland" to encourage prospective settlers. Some 300 settlers followed him to this unlikely Promised Land, spurred on by over-population and famine in Iceland. They created two main settlements, and developed a nation-state whose population rose, at its height, to some 4,000 people.

They lived off farming and fishing and hunting. Their exports were exotic and highly prized—walrus ivory, hides, furs, walrus-hide ropes, Greenland falcons, and most spectacular of all, live Polar bears, that made a terrific impact on the royal courts of Scandinavia and Europe. When Iceland's first native bishop went to Europe for his consecration in the year 1055, he marched in with a polar bear in tow, and you can imagine the sensation he made!

Time has been relatively kind to the remains of the Norsemen in Greenland. Danish archaeologists have excavated hundreds of ruined farmhouses, including the long-house of Eirik the Red himself at Brattahlid (Kagssiarssuk) and the tiny medieval chapel built nearby by his wife Thjodhild. They have also found the massive traces of the cathedral and bishopric at Gardar (Igaliko), built of red sandstone blocks with glass windows.

Today, Igaliko is a prosperous and tranquil little community of 100 people. The houses are all built of massive blocks of red sandstone quarried from the cathedral in the days before Greenland became aware of its rich historical antiquities. It was here, in fact, late in the 18th century, that the first Eskimoes were taught farming, and a series of nomadic hunting tribes began to gell into a nation.

But to return to the Norsemen. Everything went pretty well for them to start with—well enough for the European Church to want to get an oar in and establish a bishopric. The ruins at Gardar, in fact, give ample evidence of the power and wealth that the Greenlandic church was able to harness and exploit.

But then the weather began to change, disastrously, for the worse. Remember the Little Ice Age, when oxen could be roasted on the frozen Thames? In Greenland it meant a return to the cruel conditions of the Ice Age itself. The ice advanced southwards again, and with it came the hunting Eskimoes. The Norsemen, who had always been living right on the edge of possibility, couldn't cope.

Igaliko—a prosperous and tranquil little community of 100 people

Archaeological remains show that they gradually gave up husbandry and reverted to hunting themselves. Their two settlements died out—how, no one knows for sure. Perhaps by evacuation to the northern coasts of America. Perhaps wiped out by the Eskimoes (the Eskimoes would never have understood the passionate Norse attachment to land, to land-ownership, and there would almost certainly have been conflict between them).

A new book on the market tells the story of the Norsemen in Greenland with great vividness and authority. It's called *Viking Greenland,* a translation of a book by the leading Danish archaeologist there, Knud J. Krogh, and published by the National Museum of Denmark. It contains all the most up-to-date archaeological evidence, and is stunningly illustrated. The translation is by that genial war-horse of Icelandic studies, Professor Gwyn Jones of University College, Cardiff.

I had the privilege of meeting Knud Krogh and being taken round the excavations at Brattahlid by him. What a pleasure it is to meet an enthusiast! Under his spell, Brattahlid came to life again: the warm and comfortable long-hall where the household spent the winter evenings—working their wool (Greenland tweed was highly esteemed), playing chess, telling stories, and according to the Sagas, discussing the New World of Vinland in North America and the trans-Atlantic trade-routes pioneered by Eirik the Red's son, Leif the Lucky. Outside, the byre had room for 40 cows. And then, about 200 yards away, Thjodhild's chapel, built according to the Sagas at a discreet distance away, because Eirik the Red refused to be converted to Christianity. Thjodhild was, however, and refused to sleep with her husband thereafter, which annoyed the old pagan no end. No wonder.

Further down the coast, at Hvalsey (Whalsey, as in Shetland), there is the ruin of a magnificent roofless stone church. It was here that the last records of Norse Greenland peter out, with the account of a wedding that was held there in September, 1408. There's

Finding a native Greenlander who can still handle an Eskimo kayak is increasingly difficult

something intriguing about the fact that the recorded story of Greenland ends with a wedding; in all the best Lutheran stories, the ending is a wedding. It's only in Catholic stories that the beginning is a wedding—perhaps because they cannot ever get divorced!

But for modern Greenland, it's the beginning of the story again, after the centuries of silence and neglect when the cold gripped the land and Europe looked away. Today, Greenland is fast becoming *the* exotic tourist resort, for tourists who want something different—a dash of adventure, a dash of discomfort, and an experience to cap any that their friends can manage.

They ferry across from Iceland and Denmark in droves: Germans, Americans, British, intent on a four-day fiesta that brooks no opposition from Arctic mosquitos or Arctic fogs. I found their determined enthusiasm rather infectious; but I confess I'm glad I don't have to spend the winter listening to their travellers' tales.

Which, come to think of it, is just what I've been foisting on you. . . .

September, 1970

Dr Peter Harbison at Newgrange, County Meath

23

Ireland sees a Great Future
for the Past

I COULD HARDLY believe the figures. But then, figures aren't really there to be believed, only to be admired. Nonetheless, they gave me pause, as they say:

In the league table of activities or pastimes indulged in by visitors to Ireland last year, first came walking (59.2 per cent); then came general sightseeing (54.8 per cent); and third—and this is the one that gets me—third came visiting historic monuments or other sites of cultural importance: 51.2 per cent of all visitors to Ireland last year, no less.

When you consider the rather mindless way in which the majority of us console ourselves on holiday, that statistic is little short of staggering. Mind you, it is based on a market research survey in which visitors to Ireland during the summer of '71 were requested to answer a questionnaire which included the question, "Which of the following pastimes did you personally engage in? . . ." There was no heading for boozing, or ogling girls, or lying around doing nothing, all of which I suspect might have come rather high in the list. And besides, one might well feel slightly ashamed of answers of that nature, and might be tempted to paint the lily a little by putting a more respectable gloss on one's activities. Thus, "walking" could perhaps be subdivided into "walking between pubs" or "walking down the street looking for talent."

However, it is also significant that the 1,115,000 visitors from Britain weren't nearly so culturally minded as the rest : Ireland's historic monuments saw only 36.6 per cent of them, compared with 65 per cent of all Continental visitors, and a massive 75.7 per cent of all North American visitors. And *that* rings true, for sure.

But however one regards the figures, I will confess to considerable pleasure in them. For I am a sucker for ancient monumentary. I believe passionately in the value and validity of the past, and I believe that the best holidays are those which are not spent recumbent like slugs on a beach, but in purposeful pursuit of enduring interests which can reinvigorate the mind. And that is precisely what the Irish are offering—more power to them.

The Irish Tourist Board (Bord Failte) is the only tourist organisation I know of that employs, full-time, a trained archaeologist on its staff—not to conduct excavations on the Board's behalf, but to promote and co-ordinate the Board's policy where cultural and historic interests are involved. His name is Dr Peter Harbison, a man of engaging enthusiasms, whose job is also to meet overseas visitors with particularly cultural interests.

This year he has £30,000 to spend on improving amenities in his particular field—access roads to sites, sign-posts, plaques, car-parks, toilets. It's not a vast sum to invest when you consider that last year's visitors to Ireland (over half of whom visited ancient monuments) left £104 million in Irish tills; even so, it's a lot more than most tourist organizations spend. And with any luck, it's going to be an awful lot more in the years to come.

For Ireland is blest with an incredible number of magnficent mementoes of the past. All around you is a pageant of history. Successive waves of civilizations and cultures have washed over Ireland's delectable shores, and all have left their mark, not just on the character and psychology of the people but on the countryside itself. Immigrants of the Stone Age built their solemn cemeteries there, the great chambered tombs and passage-graves like Newgrange, near Dublin. The Bronze Age inhabitants left massive stone circles and an incredible legacy of prehistoric gold ornaments that now grace the National Museum. The Iron Age (600 BC onwards) left a number of impressive stone fortifications like the breath-taking Dun Aenghus on the Aran Islands. It was these self-same Celts, or Gaels, who with the advent of Christianity in the 5th century AD gave Ireland a Golden Age of art and architecture, noble church treasures like the Ardagh Chalice and illuminated manuscripts, and the magnificent High Crosses so characteristic of Celtic Christianity. The Vikings came and founded cities like Dublin and Wexford, now the site of an important opera festival every autumn. And in the 12th century the Normans arrived with their instant castles—some of which, like Bunratty Castle, have survived long enough for medieval banquets to be served in them still, every night of the week.

Dr Harbison's plans for this year include the spending of some £6,000 to provide a car-park, toilets, and recreation area at the ruined early Christian site of Monasterboice in County Louth, home of the finest of all the High Crosses of Ireland—the 10th century Cross of Muiredach with its superbly carved panels. His other major scheme is to help finance the building of a local museum at Craggaunowen in County Clare, right over in the west, to house a fine private collection of antiquities and works of art. In addition, they are planning to build reconstructions of a typical Iron Age ring-fort and a crannog (small artificial island built on stilts on the edge of a lake and defended by a wooden palisade). Visitors in the future will find a kind of prehistoric Skansen; and Dr Harbison is pouring in £15,000—one third of the eventual total cost of this imaginative tourist development.

But there are even more exciting possibilities on the horizon. They are created by two epic archaeological excavations which are going on in Ireland at present—the one at the huge prehistoric mound of Knowth, and the other in the heart of Dublin itself. Both offer tremendous opportunities for the creation of spectacular monuments that would rival some of the great attractions of the classical world.

The great mound of Knowth, some 40 feet high and almost 300 feet in diameter, is part of an extensive Stone Age cemetery in the bend of the River Boyne in County Meath. It's just as big as its more celebrated neighbour, Newgrange, but is clearly destined to become even more renowned.

Until 1962, it was Newgrange that claimed all the attention; for in its heart, at the end of a long stone passage, was a soaring burial chamber lavishly decorated with the enigmatic ornamentation of the Stone Age people who built it—whorls, spirals, lozenges, chevrons, circles. But in 1962 one of Ireland's leading archaeologists, Dr George Eogan, began to investigate the still intact mound of Knowth, for there were signs that in addition to the great mound itself, there was the possibility of two or even three smaller burial mounds grouped around it.

For four seasons Dr Eogan patiently skinned the surrounding area and the turf of the mound itself. In 1967 his patience was

Among the many fascinating sites excavated in the High Street of Dublin was a cobbler's scrap area from which was recovered a vast amount of material including the 13th century child's bootee shown opposite

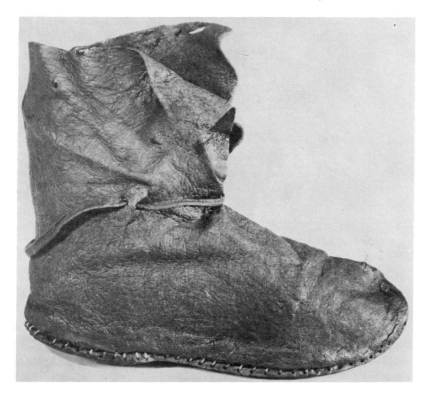

rewarded, when his systematic and painstaking study revealed a massive decorated kerb-stone with a groove across it that seemed to point the way to an entrance. And entrance it was. A stone-lined passage led into a flat-roofed chamber which had clearly been used for an important burial, more than 4,000 years ago.

In the following year came an even more spectacular discovery. As Dr Eogan worked his way round the mound, he found a second entrance. The stones of the passage leaned dangerously inward, but he inched his way through the darkness, squeezing past great stones incised with strange designs; gradually the walls began to widen, until he found himself standing in a great stone chamber whose roof towered above his head in a series of corbelled steps. It was like finding Tutankhamun's tomb, all over again.

With the extraordinary disciplined caution of the true archaeologist, Dr Eogan closed up the chamber again, for it was not ready for full-scale excavation. For the past three seasons he has been busy completing his scheduled excavation of the *outside* of the mound—and has discovered at least 17 lesser grave-mounds around it. These, after excavation, are being reconstructed in their original form, so that future visitors will be able to see the surrounding graveyard in its original state and enter all the tumuli in safety. By cutting trenches and squares on top of the great mound itself, he has also been able to lay bare the way in which succeeding peoples used the original mound for their own purposes.

Soon after the mound was built, as a centre-piece for this cemetery, the so-called Beaker people moved in with their tents, leaving fragments of their distinctive beaker pottery as the only traces of their presence. Nearly 2,000 years later, men of the Iron Age fortified it as a hill-fort, with two concentric ditches, one quite near the top, and lived in it during the centuries of turbulence. When the hill-fort people moved out, round about the 6th century AD, the early Christians moved in, and built an elaborate series of tunnels and underground hidey-holes called souterrains, which now honeycomb the sides and top of the mound. These continued in use until at least the 10th century, because two Anglo-Saxon coins of the 10th century were found in one of them. Later still, the Normans used the mound as a ready-made base for a fortified motte, which lasted till the 14th century.

This great cross-section of Irish history will all be reconstructed for the benefit of the public, if Dr Eogan has his way, just as Sir Arthur Evans left Knossos, in Crete, as a living monument for all time. But more: Ireland has a chance of linking up all the monuments of the bend of the Boyne in a National Park which would give visitors a chance of seeing them all in their proper context and relationship. The opportunity is there; and I shall be surprised if the Irish don't take it.

The Dublin dig is another splendid opportunity. Since 1962, archaeologists have been probing for the Viking city that underlies the heart of old Dublin, in the High Street area. As buildings are pulled down for redevelopment, they have been digging 14 feet down through the debris of centuries to find the houses and shops which the first Viking settlers built. They have come across a mass of magnificently preserved remains that are already the envy of Scandinavia: ornaments, tools, textiles, a comb-maker's shop, a cobbler's shop with dozens of discarded leather boots. . . . This is the side of Viking life we hear of so seldom, the Vikings who taught the west trade and commerce.

Here is a chance to make the basement of the planned new municipal chambers a living museum for visitors to Dublin, with the post-and-wattle walls still standing as the Vikings left them, the water-channels, the flagged pavements, the raw materials of the craftsmen in the very spot where they have lain for nearly a thousand years. It's an inspiring thought.

And there are no prizes for guessing which besotted latter-day Viking will be queuing up to be the first visitor when it opens.

July, 1972

24

On the Trail of an Obsession

IN THE OLD DAYS they just used to call it demoniac possession, and
hustle you off for a quick cure at the stake. Now they call it being
obsessed. Or just going batty.

Oh yes, a bad case of obsession all right. Which is ridiculous, when
you consider that the woman's been dead for nearly 50 years, and
that it's more than a hundred years since she fell in love and got
married—to someone else.

Maybe you've had obsessions like this yourselves. Anyway, as
they say when the screen goes shoogly just before the flashback
starts, it all started very, very innocently. . . .

It was just before New Year. Little did I know, etc (hell, you all
know the script, why waste your time?)

The letter was so innocent, so blandly innocuous. It came from a
friend of mine in Iceland; he's the Director of the National Museum,
and someone in Iceland had been banging his ears about something,
so he was just passing it on to get it off his back.

It was like this. The little church at Thingvellir had just been
restored to the condition it had been in a century ago. They had done
it up all nice and as-you-were; all that was needed now was to find
some of the stuff that had been in it a hundred years ago, and all
would be just perfect. Now, the church records suggested that in the
year 1899, the altarpiece, a painting that served as a reredos behind
the altar, had been sold to a tourist (except one didn't call them
tourists in those days—they were travellers); and this tourist was a
Scots lady called, they thought, "Disne Leith." And since my friend
had promised to look into it (anything to keep them quiet), could
I—would I—might I? You know the rest.

◄ Mary Gordon—Mrs Disney Leith

Nothing loth, I plunged in. It was a challenge, you see: a challenge to my patriotism, and to my journalistic snout. Especially because the fellow had cunningly said something about it being an impossible quest.

Ho ho, I'll show him, said I. And with that I was sunk.

It turned out to be relatively easy to trace this woman; I phoned the reference department of the Mitchell Library in Glasgow (much the best reference section in all Britain), and in a trice they had turned up an obituary of a Mrs Disney Leith, and a whacking great list of books she had written—including a book about her travels in Iceland. (Actually, it would have been even easier if I had phoned my Dad, because he had all her books in his bookshelves—but that would have been no fun).

So the next stage was to look for living descendants who might be able to tell what had happened to the altarpiece this woman had bought. She herself came from the Isle of Wight, but she had married an Aberdeenshire laird, Col. Disney Leith of Glenkindie, so I reckoned I ought to be able to find a few Leiths still knocking around. So I chased around in *Who's Who* and *Debrett* and *Burke's Landed Gentry* (very blue-blooded, was our Mrs Disney Leith); and eventually just looked up the Aberdeenshire telephone book, which I should have done at once, of course, and there it was. A granddaughter-in-law put me in touch with a grand-daughter, and the stage was set for one of those blood-tingling telephone calls that will prove all or nothing.

So that was how I came to phone the Hon. Miss Mildred Katherine Leith (b. March 22, 1894, e.d. 5th Baron Burgh—I had found her in *Debrett* by now, and the vernacular is catching). It must have been rather an odd experience for her, come to think of it, getting a phone call like that right out of the blue, and out of the past.

" . . . I'm doing some research on behalf of . . . was your grandmother the Mrs Disney Leith who . . . I see . . . you went to Iceland *with* her, did you? As a little girl? Six times? *Six* times, did you say? And what about your grandmother, did she go often? *Eighteen times?* Ye gods! Tell me now, Miss Leith, did you ever hear anything about an altarpiece your grandmother is said to have bought in Iceland? Yes, *altarpiece.* From the little church at a place called Thingvellir . . . You *did?* Any idea what happened to it? Any idea where it is now—you didn't inherit it, I suppose (forced laugh)?

Oh, she gave it to another church, did she? What, in Aberdeenshire? Oh, the Isle of Wight, I see. . . ."

And so it was only a question of phoning a vicarage or two (I know it was Sunday, but parsons forgive anything just after a good Sunday lunch, and they all found the question so bizarre that they got interested in it), and soon I had run it to earth in a handsome old village church at Shorwell.

And that, I thought, was that. Mission accomplished. Report back to base. Send 'em a telegram: "Altarpiece found," all mock modesty, you know the kind of thing. You can't teach an old Express reporter anything about this game, etc, etc. Just the formalities now, apply to the bishop for a sale or exchange, the thing's as good as back home where it belongs, in the little stone-and-turf church where the Icelandic nation was born. . . .

And then, to my horror, I realised that it wasn't all over at all. It was only just starting in fact. What was this woman doing in Iceland, eighteen times, at the turn of the century? What did she want to go and buy an old altarpiece for? What was she like? What drew her to Iceland, of all places? Why? Why? What was she like? Was she pretty? Tough? Eccentric? Nuts? Eighteen times, her granddaughter had said; and always on horseback. And when she was seventy years old, she had gone back, to bathe in the Arctic Sea just one more time. . . .

It was at this point that the obsession began.

It was like falling in love. I craved every crumb of information about her. I read every word she had written. I combed the reference books, local newspaper files. No lover cruelly separated from his sweetheart could have been more dismayed at the postal strike than I, for the flow of information stopped; photographs of my beloved were stuck in the post for six tantalising weeks of agony.

And then I met her. Tiny, she was, Tiny, and intrepid. Rather a nice, long face; twinkly-crinkly eyes. Marvellous.

She was born in 1840, three years after Queen Victoria came to the throne. She was a perfect child of her time; born with a silver spoon in her mouth and a golden riding crop in her hand. Father was a Bart, mama was the daughter of an earl. "Home" was a series of magnificent houses, including an 80-roomed Jacobean manor house on the Isle of Wight, a fine town house in Chelsea with gardens running right down to the Thames, and a country mansion in

Scotland. She was tiny, talented, clever, pretty, and rich; and her cousin was destined to be a famous poet: Algernon Charles Swinburne.

They grew up together, practically: he precociously intellectual but emotionally handicapped (he became a notorious alcoholic and pervert), she determined to do everything he could do, and better. She studied music and became an extremely accomplished pianist and organist. Grandmama was a talented painter—Julia Bennet, pupil and contemporary of Turner and Wilkie—and so of course Mary (did I tell you her name was Mary? Mary Charlotte Julia Gordon) became a painter too. And she rode horses like a demon, thundering all over the Isle of Wight sidesaddle, with Swinburne. When Swinburne started writing, Mary started too—and got her first novel out by the time she was 19.

And then, suddenly, at the age of 25, she got married. No, not to Swinburne—there would have been fierce opposition to that from her parents, for Swinburne was distinctly unsuitable. Her husband was a man 20 years older than she was, a giant of a man, six foot six inches tall, with a great black beard, younger son of the laird of Glenkindie, a soldier and a hero.

The siege of Moultan, at which Col. Disney Leith lost an arm and won a reputation

In 1849, at the siege of Moultan during the Second Sikh War, the young giant, Disney Leith, led a hopeless assault on the walls of the fort. He swung himself up to the parapets with his sword clenched in his teeth. A defender sliced off his left arm with a sabre; but Disney Leith steadied himself, snatched his own sword, and clove the fellow to the brisket (I quote from the *Aberdeen Express*, I promise you). Another swarthy attacker got him on the right elbow, but Disney Leith had his head practically off in a trice, and held on until the rest of his men arrived. He had a bullet in the right shoulder by then as well. The assault succeeded, Moultan was taken, and Disney Leith came home armless but a hero. And in 1865 he married Mary Charlotte Julia Gordon.

I reckon she must have been in love with him. I refuse to believe it was a fix. She wanted someone big to dominate her. And so he did. They had six children, and Mrs Disney Leith wrote nearly a dozen novels, as well as screeds of poetry. And sometimes during that period, she got the bug about Iceland, from reading the first translations of the Sagas. And promptly taught herself Icelandic for good measure from an Icelandic-Latin dictionary.

And no sooner was the gallant Disney Leith in his grave in 1892, than Mrs Disney Leith ups and visits Iceland. She was 54 years old; and for her, life was about to start again.

Eighteen times she went to Iceland. Always travelling on horseback. Writing her diary religiously every night, fording raging glacier rivers, dreaming of the heroic past of the Sagas, lovingly describing this strange new world of cultivated peasants that was so totally different from the aristocratic world of landed gentry she had always known.

As a devout Anglo-Catholic, she was particularly interested in everything to do with the Icelandic church. Secretly she hoped for a Catholic revival in that staunchly Lutheran and pagan land. She even organised a little monument to the last Catholic bishop of Iceland, a reckless nationalist who had been beheaded by the Danes as part of the Reformation: what they call martyrdom if you're on the right side.

And then, in 1898, her younger son died; he was a soldier, and it happened in India. Mrs Disney Leith wrote a passionate poem of Lament; and the following year she went back to Iceland to find solace.

She went to the heart of the country, to Thingvellir, where the Icelandic nation had been born in the year 930, the awesome site of Iceland's ancient open-air Parliament. There had been a little church there since the dawn of Christianity. And now she asked the pastor if she might buy the altarpiece, for her son had seen it and admired it so much in 1894.

And she bought it. It was a painting, some two feet by three, of the Last Supper: a remarkably naïve, even primitive painting, made by a local crofter in 1835. A painting on a couple of panels of driftwood stuck together. A humble thing, but full of reverence.

And she bought it. And brought it back to Britain, and gave it to the little church at Shorwell where she had worshipped all her childhood. And she dedicated it to the memory of her son, Robert Thomas Disney Leith. And there it hung for all those years, this rather baffling piece of church furniture, covered with incomprehensible Icelandic lettering (it was the story of the Last Supper in Gothic printing). Until someone in Iceland said, "I wonder what happened to that altarpiece they used to have in Thingvellir Church?" . . .

It's back in Iceland now, thanks to the generosity of the Shorwell congregation, and hanging once again in its proper place in Thingvellir Church. The National Museum of Iceland had a replica made, and presented it to Shorwell.

And I am still left with a marvellous obsession, about a little old lady called Mary Disney Leith.

August, 1971